GENESIS:
The Book of Beginnings

GENESIS:
The Book of Beginnings

DAVID A. LEACH

Judson Press® Valley Forge

GENESIS: THE BOOK OF BEGINNINGS
Copyright © 1984
Judson Press, Valley Forge, PA 19482-0851

Bible quotations in this volume are from *The New English Bible*. Copyright © The Del-
egates of the Oxford University Press and The Syndics of the Cambridge University
Press 1961, 1970.

Library of Congress Cataloging in Publication Data
Leach, David A.
   Genesis, the book of beginnings.

   1. Bible.   O.T.   Genesis—Criticism, interpretation, etc. I. Title.
BS1235.2.L34   1984   222'.1106   84-12271
ISBN 0-8170-1047-5

The name JUDSON PRESS is registered as a trademark in the U.S. Patent Office.
Printed in the U.S.A. ⊕

This book is dedicated to my father, the late R. F. Leach, whose commonsense approach to Scripture and the Christian gospel inspired this particular study and much of my approach to the Christian ministry.

Contents

Introduction

When we consider society's attitude toward the Bible, we identify one of the enigmas of our culture. The Bible is a best seller. It is revered and worshiped. It is carried at weddings, read at funerals, and generally treated as a good luck charm. Yet it is not read with any great consistency. Its contents are only vaguely known. A large percentage of our populace is painfully ignorant of its major themes. In short, nearly everyone owns a copy, very few read it, and even fewer understand it. Perceived as a book with magical potency, the Bible is placed on a shelf and ignored.

Because the Bible is believed to be the Word of God (whatever that may mean), some persons occasionally attempt to read it. The individual picks it up and logically begins with the beginning, Genesis 1:1. Since he or she has had no preparation, after only a few chapters the individual sets the Bible aside. A feeling of failure and a vague sense of guilt remain. After all, one *should* read the Bible. However, struggling with the "begat" sections, as well as a few of the more confusing traditions from ancient culture, can lead one into a stage of bewilderment.

That it shouldn't be this way is fairly obvious. Reading

the Word of God should be exciting. If the living God loves us, as the church has proclaimed, what the Bible has to tell us can only be for our edification and personal growth. To be involved in communication with One who loves us should not be confusing, nor should it be threatening. Still, not everyone is convinced that God is a God of love. One's early religious training may have given one an ambiguous message, at best. At worst, it may have taught about a terribly judgmental and vindictive God. We must ask such a person to reexamine the revelation of God in Jesus Christ before reading the remainder of the Bible because it is only then that he or she will see any clear meaning or consistency.

Then there is the problem of listening as a part of the communication process. We have too often assumed listening to be a simple matter of assimilating the verbalized message. When this simple procedure is accepted as all there is to listening, serious problems result. Certainly such a procedure will not result in greater closeness between two persons. Different settings give different meanings to the same words. A change of tone or volume or an altered facial expression will change the meaning of the same words or phrases for the one listening. Further, the verbal message changes depending on who is delivering it. If I am listening to my employer, my teacher, my spouse, my friend, or my parent, the words will take on a particular flavor.

Unfortunately, the complexities of listening have largely been ignored in the approach to the Bible. Most people have approached the Bible in a very pedestrian fashion. Verse by verse they plod along, occasionally checking a dictionary meaning but never allowing for the totality of the message or its personal quality to come through.

What we as persons living in the present want and need from our Bible reading is to receive a message from a personal God. That is a large order. I would not want to minimize the complexity. However, I see the Bible as being just this: an instrument through which we as persons of our time can be in touch with the will and purpose of this living God.

This brings us back to the first book of the Bible where

our frustrated reader began. As we begin to listen to God speak through Genesis, we begin to hear messages that are remarkably relevant to contemporary living. Our most important concern is to discover how we can live on this crowded planet without destroying ourselves and each other. That spells community. The book of Genesis describes humanity's beginning efforts at building community. Here is demonstrated humanity's failure to find creative ways to cope with individual differences.

And we go right on making the same mistakes! Instead of cooperating, we compete. Instead of showing concern for our neighbors, we ignore them. Instead of listening to them, we shout them down. Our own needs loom so large that we have no time or energy left to look at those of anyone else. By failing to hear the message clearly outlined in the book of Genesis, we move on toward our own destruction.

Look again through this significant bit of literature. Listen as God speaks through these words. Listen as God calls a people into being and in the process reveals much of himself. Be aware as God shows us what we are meant to be. Hear just how contemporary these ancient words can be. You will find challenge and inspiration if you will only open your eyes and unstop your ears.

One warning is in order. The discussion that follows is meant to be a beginning. It is an invitation for you to return to the book of Genesis to find further meaning and particular guidance for your own life. No one of us will exhaust the meaning in a lifetime. Feel with me the excitement of this remarkable book of the Bible. Struggle with me as we read again the Book of Beginnings.

Questions for Reflection

1. What has been your experience in reading the Bible? the book of Genesis?

2. Examine your attitude toward the Bible. Think back

through early family, church school, and worship experiences that shaped your attitude. List those influences which determined whether you now worship the Bible or the God of the Bible.

3. Before reading the book of Genesis, take some time to be in touch with the feelings you have about the book. How many people in the book can you name? What images come to mind when you think of these people? What characteristics did they have that remind you of people you know today?

4. Consider the complexity of the listening process as it relates to the communication between you and your contemporaries. List those elements of listening you will need to take to the experience of reading Genesis.

5. What would it mean to you to have God speak to you through the book of Genesis? Identify any barriers you might have to the listening process.

1

Retreat to the Brush

Genesis 1–3

The first three chapters of Genesis have attracted as much printer's ink as any other passages of Scripture. Though written with a simple poetic beauty, they have spawned enormous controversy and no little confusion. Much of the problem stems from attempts to prove the accounts to be literally true in every detail. Unfortunately, while the controversy goes on, the truth is lost. For this passage of Scripture to have contemporary meaning, the basic truths have to be uncovered.

If the title of the book has any meaning (and that seems a fairly valid assumption), any basic truth contained in it will be concerned with beginnings, since the meaning of the Greek root of "Genesis" is "beginning." Certainly this is a genuine interest. How did the world get here? Where did I come from? These are questions asked in every generation and in every culture. Myths, legends, fables, and theories have all been set forth to answer these questions of origin. So if we are reading a book entitled "Genesis," we would expect it to give us some answers to these questions, especially when its opening statements are aimed at doing just that in broad and general terms.

The beginning point is God—God's activity. "In the beginning God created . . . " is a statement of fact. There is no proof given; it is just stated. As a result of God's creative art, time began and the world came into existence. For those who have experienced a living God, this explanation is all that is necessary. For those who have not, nothing would be sufficient. This fact does not invite speculative discussion or arguments concerning scientific issues but makes a statement to those with faith commitments. The earth is the Lord's because he created it. Now we must discover what God's intentions were for it.

Without getting bogged down, then, in arguments concerning the literal account, we must look for the important lessons. Looked at closely, these lessons begin to surface and show a contemporary importance. God has created a world in which there is order. Although the threat of chaos is continuing, God is sovereign and ordains order. With that order comes balance and interdependence.

The importance of interdependence becomes apparent from the very beginning of Genesis. The authors and editors were not heavily committed to the *details* of creation. There simply is not much space given to the account. A few short verses dispense with the creation of the earth. The important concern is with the creation of man. "Man" means the human race—male and female—and a major concern is with humanity, corporately.

As we read on, we soon find ourselves involved with the style and problems of relationship. Human beings are expected to relate to the earth and animals in a certain way. They are expected to interrelate with God and with those of their own kind. Their failures to find the right way to interrelate become the primary thrust and the main burden of the narrative. Out of this comes a revelation of the potential of human beings, their reason for existing and also their predicament. The interdependence of humanity with God is the way God intended it to be. Since a true interdependence is rooted in the freedom of both parties, we now look at humanity's response. Does humanity choose interdependence or independence from God?

All of this comes into focus in the account of the Fall. The opening scene is a picture of tranquility. God has created Adam and Eve and placed them in an idyllic setting. They are given a responsibility: "Be fruitful and increase, fill the earth, and subdue it, rule over the fish in the sea, the birds of the heaven, and every living thing that moves upon the earth" (1:28). Though the two accounts of the creation (1:1–2:4 and 2:5-25) differ in detail, the relationship between God and humanity remains constant. God is the Creator; humanity is the creation. Yet, strangely, there is a sharing of responsibility. The harmony is to be maintained by humanity's acceptance of a responsibility within the outline given by God. Humanity is free to choose a life of responsible interdependence with God or a life of independence, cut off from God in denial of God's sovereignty.

How humanity chooses and what is done with this responsibility makes for a remarkable little drama. Act I finds God relating freely to Adam and Eve. As a part of that relationship, God puts into the middle of the scene a curious tree (the like of which has never been seen since—"the tree of the knowledge of good and evil"). Act II finds Adam and Eve facing a choice with regard to that tree. They are warned by God of fearful consequences if they should eat of the fruit of it. With "help" from the serpent they choose to disobey. Act III is the confrontation between God and "man" and a beginning outline of resulting consequences.

In our attempts to put flesh on the bare bones of this drama, several interpretive possibilities present themselves. We can be very pedestrian and literal. This could allow for lengthy and involved arguments concerning the nature of the tree of the knowledge of good and evil. Could it have been an apple tree? Maybe it was a peach tree. Then there is the serpent. A talking snake is a bit difficult to visualize. Rather clearly, a literal approach raises questions that do not lead to contemporary challenge and inspiration.

Leaving out the fruit tree for the moment, let's consider

how we could explain the serpent. One response would be simply to dismiss the entire incident. The idea of a talking snake is so far outside of my frame of reference that my mind cannot handle it. Unfortunately, if I choose that response, the remainder of the passage loses its value for me as well.

A second response is to see the talking serpent as a phenomenon occurring on that one occasion. At the beginning of human history the snake could stand upright and converse with humans. Utilizing his powers of communication, the snake approached Adam and Eve with certain suggestions. In listening to the snake and acting on one of its suggestions, Adam and Eve found themselves guilty before God. Because of the snake's complicity in the event, it suffered the loss of communication with humans and was condemned to slide on its belly for the rest of time.

This choice isn't much more attractive than the first. This explanation attributes to the serpent the choice to tempt Adam and Eve. Again, this leaves me with too many loose ends. I have no clue as to the snake's motivation. I do not understand why Adam and Eve should listen to it. Since a snake no longer has a voice box and does not represent an attractive quality for me, how can I understand its ability to tempt?

Therefore, let's consider the third possibility for interpretation and the one that has the most meaning for me. Though it doesn't come from a clearly identifiable source outside of myself, I have had experience with a spirit that has prompted me to be something other than that which I was created to be. Something (or someone) has pushed me toward being a super achiever beyond my human capacity. At various times I have experienced urges to be super generous or super righteous beyond my capabilities. As a result of these experiences, I can understand the serpent's action in this narrative. Seen in this way the serpent becomes a symbol for that demonic power with which I have had some experience. This makes it possible for me to be open to the main message of the story.

If we are listening to a personal God speak in these words,

we can see a clear emphasis upon the relational. The main issue is not with fruit trees or talking snakes. The main issue concerns our relationship with God and with each other. Humanity was given freedom to fulfill a role in the midst of God's creation. We are free to be fully human in the context of God's sovereignty. By attempting to be *more* than human ("like gods" —see 3:5), Adam and Eve became *less* than human. The "less than human" became evident in a later alienation from each other.

Let us underscore certain biblical statements that are especially important to any understanding of the term "human" as it comes from the Bible. The answer to the "Who am I?" question begins right here. Fittingly enough, our special attention centers in the first chapter. Foundational statements should come at the beginning.

The statements concern God's announcement of intent to create humankind and an announcement of the fulfillment of that intention. In 1:26, "Let us make man in our image and likeness to rule . . . ," there is an emphasis upon humanity's nature and purpose. The phrase "our image and likeness" clearly puts the nature of this part of creation in focus. Obviously, "image" cannot mean appearance and physical attributes. The struggle of the disciples (especially Thomas and Philip) in the fourteenth chapter of John provides a commentary. The special creation—humanity—is to be able to share in God's rule over the remainder of creation. "Image" has to do with a capacity to relate to God on a special level that still permits freedom of choice.

The statement of the accomplishment of humanity's creation is likewise illuminating. In 1:27, we read, "So God created man in his own image; in the image of God he created him; male and female he created them." "Man" is made up of two individual types called "male" and "female." In another tradition recorded in the second chapter, there is a seeming contradiction but only in the *method* of creation. The statement " 'It is not good for the man to be alone . . . '" emphasizes the intent of God to fulfill his purpose in diversity. As the remainder of the narrative unfolds, it becomes clear that being human means being male and female living in community.

This simplified interpretation can be the foundation from which a more complex and meaningful understanding of human life can emerge. In order to react to this increased understanding, we must focus on the broad dimension of human responsibility and culpability. Looking more closely at the sin involved, we get a new feeling for the question of sin itself. The temptation concerns "the tree of the knowledge of good and evil." That phrase doesn't clarify what the temptation was until we look more closely at the attraction described in the narrative. If Adam and Eve eat of the fruit, they will become "like God." If they succumb to the temptation, the difference between God and humanity could be eliminated.

So what is the danger involved in this? We now connect to a major theme of the entire Bible. To be fully human (and, therefore, alive), members of humanity must live in love. Jesus said that the greatest of the commandments, and the fulfillment of all of them, is love. Humans are to love God and their neighbors. Love has its roots in freedom. If love is coerced or even automatic, it is not love. The freedom to choose and the necessity for choice are related to the maintenance of separateness and differences between the two parties loving each other.

Seen in this light, other factors begin to fit. If the separateness between God and humanity becomes blurred by the human attempt to become like God, something also happens to the separateness between individual humans. Instead of a cooperative approach to fulfilling their purpose—to rule over the earth—competition, suspicion, and guilt enter in. Without a recognition of God's sovereignty, no interdependence is possible and disorder threatens.

So humanity was confronted by a choice. The first choice was to accept the incompleteness of being male and female and create a new kind of wholeness by the exercise of love. Choosing love and creating this new wholeness would have issued in a world of peace and harmony. Differences would not have been a threat in that world, but all individuality would have been allowed appropriate expression.

But Adam and Eve (and humanity) made a second choice. By eating the fruit of the tree of the knowledge of good and evil, they made the choice to be "like God" and repudiate their created nature. Though made individually, their choices had corporate consequences for humanity. Adam and Eve now saw themselves as naked. They saw themselves as separate and distinct entities. Instead of being "man," they were now male and female, leaving them vulnerable because they were terribly alone. They were forced to cover their differences, and any attempts to create community and life together would result in pain and suffering.

An important feature of this account concerns God's action following humanity's failure. Adam immediately went into hiding. He was afraid to face God and ran away. God came looking for Adam. Here is good news. God's redemptive spirit is introduced (and with it the entire theme of salvation history) in that question to Adam: "Where are you?" (3:9). Certainly the question is not one of geography, and, just as certainly, it is the question asked of humanity in every age. Where is each human in relationship to God, to his or her neighbor, to the world? In fear, suspicion, and guilt he or she has retreated into the brush. Out there he or she is lost and alone.

So as we look at this Genesis account, the "beginning" that is being described is more than a mere historical record. This is the beginning of awareness for that segment of God's creation called "human." To become aware of human potential and personal abilities is to face choice. Choice, to have any validity, implies freedom, and when we exercise that freedom, we face the consequences. Individually, we must face our own beginning—that time when we become responsibly self-conscious. It is then that we choose what we will be.

What we are saying is that a heavy emphasis upon the historicity of Adam and Eve may simply be an excuse for avoiding our own point of origin. Maintaining such an emphasis may mean that we are clinging to innocence, resulting in nonpersonhood, or that we are unwittingly expressing our own guilt and fear and doing our own hiding in the brush. To come to grips with this part of the Bible is to live through it and to acknowledge its challenge to us personally. To get the most from this passage is to hear God calling us into personhood.

So how do we put ourselves into the story? Our surroundings hardly classify as the Garden of Eden and we may not have been confronted by a talking snake. Still, it isn't difficult to identify our life situation. For all of us there has been something within us challenging us. It has to do with self-worth and personal significance. Who am I? This is the first question and the basic issue in our nagging need for self-fulfillment.

When we face this challenge, we find our identity with Adam and Eve. From this point God's message takes on new clarity. Who am I? I am God's creation. I have been created incomplete in and of myself. I must be related to others in God's creation. That relationship must come as a result of free choice. Freely chosen, the relationship is an expression of love. Love makes community possible. To be me as God intended me to be is to live in community.

Looking at this in the most pragmatic sense is hearing God emphasize "male and female created he them." The family is the beginning of human fulfillment. It is the symbol and model for all that follows. The family begins with separateness, distinctness, freedom of choice, and love. Each member begins by owning his or her own feelings. Each member must face the personal consequences of a wrong choice.

The human begins life with a fairly lengthy period of dependency. The struggle is toward independence. With the achievement of independence comes an awareness of separation. One is naked: different, separate, vulnerable. One can't go back to childish dependence. The only creative solution is interdependence, but how is that achieved without the personal destruction that can occur during the painful stages of independence?

It is little wonder that anxiety afflicts all of us. We make choices that express our independence only to discover results other than those we expected. Instead of fulfillment and joy, pain and alienation enter our lives. Rather than dealing with this pain and alienation directly, we hide in the brush.

It is out of this situation of alienation and lost innocence that humans are called into community. God will not allow us to remain in the brush. God will seek "Adam" out and confront him. In that confrontation there will be a redemptive experience as humanity redefines roles and chooses to acknowledge a basic incompleteness and need. Here is the beginning of the grace of God at work.

Questions for Reflection

1. How do the two accounts of creation differ in detail? How do you respond to the fact that they differ? If you feel a need to defend the differences between them, how will you proceed with your defense?

2. The first account of creation appearing in Genesis 1:1–2:4 clearly sees humanity as the crown of creation: " . . . in the image of God he created [them]." How would you define "image of God" as it pertains to humanity, including that part of humanity which is your own person?

3. The second account of creation appearing in Genesis 2:5-25 at first glance seems to be quite different from the first. Instead of being created in God's image, humanity, like the animals, is formed from the dust of the earth. In your own self-awareness what evidence do you find within yourself of a dual nature of "image of God" and "dust of the earth"? In what ways do you find your actions and attitudes reflecting these two natures?

4. Jesus uses the statement of 2:24 in response to a question concerning divorce (see Mark 10:1-9). In the light of the statement that Eve was created from Adam's flesh, what does it mean to become "one flesh"? In what way is the sequence of separation and reuniting operative today?

5. If you ever listened to an inner urge and made a choice to be less than that for which you were created, how did you experience your surroundings afterward? In what ways did your environment go from "pleasant" to "cursed"?

6. In their guilt over having eaten of the tree of the knowledge of good and evil, Adam and Eve hid in the brush. With your own experience of guilt what hiding places have you utilized? In your attempts at projection ("'The woman you gave me for a companion . . . '") and rationalization ("'The serpent tricked me . . . '") what were the results?

7. In the choice of Adam and Eve to eat of the fruit of the tree with their subsequent loss of innocence, what connection can you make with Jesus' words in Matthew 18:1-3 and his statement to Nicodemus in John 3:3-8?

2

My Brother's Keeper

Genesis 4

Nearly everyone has heard of Adam and Eve, and nearly everyone has heard of Cain and Abel. Just as the fate of Adam and Eve is common knowledge, so is that of Cain and Abel. Cain was the first murderer, and Abel was his victim. To make the crime even more reprehensible, they were brothers.

No matter how we look at this story, we will not find great beauty. The story of Cain and Abel can be seen as the rationale for the third brother's carrying on the family line. One of the emerging people of God had to carry the responsibility for maintaining the relationship with God. This became Seth by default. Cain, in a fit of anger, blew his chance to become an important part of a great tradition.

We could also approach the story with a view to what happens in unhealthy homes. When children go wrong, it is fashionable to point the finger at the parents. At first glance people may be tempted to do this. Adam and Eve did give evidence of some communication difficulties, and when defending their sinful action before God, each was inclined to avoid personal responsibility. Their accusations of each other at that time quite likely caused suspicion and serious problems. Unfortunately, the account does not go beyond their communication problems to delineate parental responsibility. Placing the blame on the parents entirely does not appear to be very helpful for our understanding. We will need to look further.

The setting for the criminal action is not too clear. We have only limited knowledge of the two men. Cain was the eldest. He was "a tiller of the soil." Abel was a shepherd. Both brought offerings to the Lord. Abel's offering was accepted; Cain's offering was rejected. Cain became angry at the rejection and murdered his brother.

Following the murder, Cain was confronted by God. As in the Adam and Eve account, it was God who forced the confrontation. God asked Adam the very significant question "Where are you?" God asked Cain another great question that will never lose its power: "Where is your brother?" The two questions go together with a poignancy that is inescapable.

Finding reasons for this crime is not as simple as it seems. The first point concerns Cain's anger. For a person to be angry enough to kill a brother, something intensely serious must be involved. Cain's anger was related to jealousy. God had accepted Abel's offering and not his. Rather than clarifying the problem with God, he killed Abel.

What was the difference in the two offerings? To say that God's acceptance of Abel's offering was due to its being a blood sacrifice is to read in something not in the text. Both brothers brought offerings of their particular produce. The text adds a significant note to the description of Abel's: "Abel brought some of the first-born of his flock, *the fat portions of them*" (4:4, author's emphasis). Abel had given some thought to his offering and apparently treated his worship with more respect than did Cain. Rather than deal responsibly with his problem, Cain angrily chose to eliminate the one who had pointed up the poor quality of his offering.

But Cain could not deceive God or hide from him. God confronted Cain with that awful question, "Where is your brother?" and got a rather strange reply: "Am I my brother's keeper?" It was meant to be evasive and was a denial of responsibility. God was not fooled, and judgment was pronounced. Cain was no longer to be a member of the family. God said, "You shall be a vagrant and a wanderer on the earth" (4:12), and so Cain was cut off from the people of God.

In considering this experience, we again recognize the biblical emphasis upon relationship and the necessity of a particular order in relationship. Each human is personally responsible to God. One's life experience begins with responsible worship. To use an old-fashioned term, if one is not right with God, one will not be right with one's brother or sister. The opposite is also a biblical emphasis. If one is not right with one's brother or sister, that is clear evidence that one is not right with God. The elder brother in the story of the prodigal makes this point clearly. The same emphasis is present in the First Epistle of John (See 1 John 4:19-20). At issue is the problem of community. To get along with our brothers and sisters, we must know where we are with God. The sovereignty of God is the foundation for peace on earth and for the emergence of community.

Another thought that comes out of this account concerns the punishment meted out to Cain. God *pronounces* what will be; he doesn't necessarily *order* it. When Cain protested that his punishment was too great, God offered a word of comfort. Without rescinding the condition of being cut off, God did offer protection for him. God does not act on the basis of the principle of an "eye for an eye and a tooth for a tooth." It seems as if the punishment is inherent in the crime and God acts to lessen the burden of punishment. In a rather primitive way, there is God's grace at work.

As with the story of Adam and Eve, the story of Cain and Abel offers an example of the difficulty in building community. Individual humans are different. Adam and Eve were "male" and "female," and Cain and Abel had different vocations. Cain was "a tiller of the soil," and Abel was "a shepherd." The differences became instruments of divisiveness. Competition and hatred resulted and community was destroyed. A lesson here may be that individual differences apart from the individuals' responsible acknowledgment of the sovereignty of God will always pose a threat.

To hear God speak to us through this account is to look at the structure of our society. Everywhere we see the type of difference that was apparent between Cain and Abel. The struggle between cowboys and farmers in our country's frontier days is legendary. Labor and management provide continual newspaper copy about negotiations that are acrimonious to the point of economic disaster. Interdisciplinary problems abound in any large university, too often resulting in a lack of communication, which, in turn, is detrimental to essential research.

On and on it goes. Examples come to mind from the experiences of all of us. Nation against nation, people against people, class against class is the order of our society and the name of the game.

Wherever differences exist there is the potential for creativity. The God who is love wants us to relate to him. In that relationship we take on God's nature and express it in the world. With that nature within us, we create community.

With God's love within us we have first of all an appreciation for the other person's worth. We do not assume a responsibility *over* the other person but demonstrate a willingness to live *with* the other person. Competition growing out of power struggles must give place to cooperation and sharing. "Keepers" turn into brothers and sisters.

So Cain murdered his brother and was confronted by God. Rather than confess and ask for pardon, he denied responsibility. His reply was a painful one, for it revealed the kind of ignorance that is still prevalent today. He asked, "Am I my brother's keeper?" Keepers are for animals in zoos. Brothers are for being brothers with and for living with—in community. God is still asking the whereabouts of our "brothers" and "sisters." It may be that unless we know who our Father is, we can never give a satisfactory answer.

Questions for Reflection

1. There are those who raise the question "Where did Cain get his wife?" The answer I would have to give is "I

don't know." Though the details are not supplied, I can
see several possibilities. If such a question is very important to you, what does that say about your attitude
toward the Bible? How does the answer or lack of it affect
your relationship to God?

2. In 4:19-24 we can read a description of a society being
   formed. Cain's crime forced him from the family of God.
   With herdsmen, artists, musicians, and craftsmen the
   community seemed complete. What can we learn from
   Lamech's statement (vv. 23 and 24) about that which
   would prevent this from becoming a true community?
   What echoes of this do you hear from today's society?

3. How do we express responsible worship? If you hear
   echoes of this chapter in Romans 12:1, how are you chal-
   lenged personally?

4. If we're not to be our "brother's keeper," what is our
   responsibility toward our brother or sister?

5. Through the act of creation we are called to participate
   in the family of God. In what ways does Cain compare
   with the elder brother in the parable of the prodigal son
   (Luke 15:11-32)?

3

Of Floods and Towers

Genesis 5:1–11:9

It would be my guess that the first four chapters of Genesis are among the most often read chapters of the Bible. My explanation for this comes from the fact that people leave the Bible lying around for long periods of time without reading it. When the guilt becomes heavy enough, they pick the Bible up and begin reading. Because of the long interim they have forgotten where they left off; so they begin again from the beginning. This new enthusiasm is usually good for about four chapters.

It just may be that fatigue is not the only factor. Chapters 5 through 11 of Genesis may be a part of the problem in that they simply are not very interesting reading. There is no consistent story line. The chapters contain long passages of genealogy. There are passages that are jarring to the modern reader. Yet, for all of the obstacles, these chapters contain some passages that carry tremendous significance for our contemporary society.

Most unnerving of the problems for a modern reader is that of lengthy genealogies. Long lists of names never make interesting reading, or else the telephone directory would be a best seller. Add to this the fact that the names are simply unfamiliar—names such as Enosh, Kenan, and Mahalalel.

Another reason why genealogies are not popular reading is that they are not important to us today. Keeping these records made sense to the ancients but makes little sense to us. In those days the maintenance of a family line through the eldest son was an important consideration. This account shows the line being maintained. Hardly of heavy importance to us today, chapter 5 could, and perhaps should, be skimmed. That would get us more quickly into something of more significance for our contemporary situation.

Another very familiar narrative unfolds in chapters 6, 7, 8, and 9. The story of Noah and the flood is well known to those who have had any church school experience at all. It is known in its simplest form as the judgment of God upon a sinful people, with a rainbow of promise as the final message. As such it is fairly easy to digest. More difficulty emerges with closer examination of the story.

The problems start early in the narrative.

> When the Lord saw that man had done much evil on earth and that his thoughts and inclinations were always evil, he was sorry that he had made man on earth, and he was grieved at heart (6:5-6).

The phrase that gives us trouble is the one referring to God's feelings of remorse: ". . . He was sorry that he had made man on earth, and he was grieved at heart." Attributing this feeling to God appears to be making God too human. This is a point not resolved for us. Though it leaves us hanging, the narrative does, however, emphasize the low point in human experience. It leaves God in charge and shows his choice to do something about the situation. We can easily believe that humanity had sunk that far; and we can understand God's decision. The important issue is not God's anger at humanity but his choice to save the race through one faithful man. Struggling too long over feelings that seem beneath God prevents us from looking at the ark and at the rainbow. Though having every right to wipe out humanity, God chose to preserve creation.

The next problem occurs when we get into the details about the size of the ark. To spend excessive energy in proving that the ark was large enough to handle the load is to miss the important issue once again. The ark was built by Noah at the command of God. Among other meanings, the ark represents the cooperation between God and humanity that ensures the continuing emergence of God's people. It is a tangible expression of one man's faithfulness and what that can mean to all of humanity. The fact that humanity deserves to be judged is evident to us all. We need the further reminder that God can do great saving acts through one faithful human being.

Another important lesson is that this faithful man did not have to be perfect to be God's instrument. The end of the story is anticlimactic at best. Noah got drunk and made a spectacle of himself. Two sons, Shem and Japheth, took pains to protect him. Ham, the third son, did not display the same concern. When Noah sobered up, he was so angry at Ham that he placed a curse on Canaan. With a strange perversity some readers ascribe this action to God and can find in this passage an excuse for racism. With just a bit more care in reading, they would discover that God was not involved in pronouncing judgment. Seldom has a man with a hangover created such a disaster.

Chapter 10 is another of those passages that deserves quick reading. The genealogies have little or no value to the contemporary reader. We can recognize this chapter to be a point of transition. The genealogies are to prepare us for the problem to be addressed in the following chapter. The earth was full of people once more, but community was still not a reality.

Chapter 11 is a beautiful synopsis of the human problem. It begins with all of humanity speaking the same language. It ends with humanity in the midst of a massive communication problem. In the middle is a description of an effort to rebuild a city. We can see that the human race began with great potential and that through technology and skill tremendous accomplishments are made. Yet, in the area of most importance—that of building community—human history is littered with failures. How do we account for this?

When we look more closely at this chapter, some clues emerge. The narrative begins with a description of simple living; people spoke one language and used the same words. Then ambition set in and plans were made to build a city. It wasn't to be just a place to allow commerce and mutuality of concern while persons lived in proximity to each other. The very language describes this attempt at human fulfillment apart from God:

> "Come," they said, "let us build ourselves a city and a tower with its top in the heavens, and make a name for ourselves; or we shall be dispersed all over the earth" (11:4).

Here is a slightly different version of the tree with the fruit of the knowledge of good and evil. We see humanity as a strong mixture of anxiety and ambition. The need to build a tower that reaches to the heavens and a need to make a name for oneself is more than just a little familiar to those who observe contemporary human expressions.

How does a human being give expression to the ambition that is a part of one's nature? How does one deal with anxiety? Though the answers are not given in this chapter, the questions are raised with a poignancy that prepares us for their full answer in Jesus Christ. This chapter does not say that it is right or wrong to build cities and towers but that they had better be built under God's direction and with an acknowledgment of his sovereignty. Otherwise, we can expect a confusion of tongues.

What one word describes our human problem today? Communication. If we put this chapter with chapter 2 of Acts, we gain remarkable insight. Where the Spirit of God dwells, there is the freedom to communicate. True community—the answer to human anxiety—can be the result of God's entrance into the world.

Questions for Reflection

1. Check your feeling response as you reflect on the statement that some passages of Scripture (genealogies) are

not very interesting reading and that they "make little sense to us." If your response is primarily negative, what does that say about your expectation in reading the Bible?

2. As you consider the account of the flood, clarify your own feelings and beliefs about the relationship of evil (or righteousness) and natural disasters. If you believe God uses earthquakes, hurricanes, and volcanic explosions to punish the unrighteous, what do you do with the experience of Job and how do you interpret Luke 13:1-5 and John 9:1-37?

3. The implication is that Noah could choose to be out of step with his culture in order to be in step with God. To what extent are you willing to be seen as strange by your friends and neighbors (see Romans 12:2)?

4. List some examples of groups attempting to "make a name for themselves" or to become "Number 1." In what way is the principle demonstrated by the story of the people of Babel valid in these examples? What signs of a breakdown in communication are evident in these examples?

4

Introduction to a Man of Faith

Genesis 11:10–15

Even a cursory reading of Genesis shows chapter 12 to be a turning point. Here is a new beginning. The tone changes; the emphasis is different. The first eleven chapters contain brief vignettes of a wide range of events and people. From chapter 12 to the end of the book we have in-depth biographical material. We can get to know the characters and recognize them as fellow humans. No longer do we have to struggle to determine the mythological meaning. These are real people with obvious meaning for real people of any age. Their social and cultural environments may be different from ours, but their minds function like ours. Their emotions are like ours, sometimes distressingly so. Their life patterns are recognizably similar to those of our contemporaries.

The first of the characters to be introduced and developed for us is Abraham. Since he was the father of three great religions, we would expect his biographers to treat him with awe. They do not. He emerges as human. At no time is he treated as someone otherworldly or super pious. Reflecting his culture, he can rise above it, but he does so in a way that presents a model to every person who would live by faith, regardless of the age in which that person lives.

The introduction to Abraham reflects the age from which the narrative comes. The story sounds quite ordinary. Following the account of the Tower of Babel, there is a transition passage that uses a genealogical table (11:10-25). Fortunately, this genealogy is brief and its purpose is clear. Its purpose is to show that the line of God's people extends from Shem to a man named Terah. Our attention is directed to the firstborn of this man's three children. The fact that the other two are even mentioned is remarkable. It becomes our first clue to the greater detail that will mark the treatment of the major characters who will appear from this point to the end of the book. It also serves to introduce Lot, who will play a fairly strong supporting role in the drama to come.

The line of the people of God moves from Shem to Terah. It includes a list of names that are not likely to become household words in the twentieth century. We move quickly through the list to Terah, who lived in Ur. Terah heard the call of God to move on. He arrived at Haran with his son Abraham, his daughter-in-law Sarah, and a nephew named Lot. He settled there and died there.

The stage is now set for perhaps the first of the truly pivotal passages of the Bible. This is the call to Abraham that tells him to set forth. As recorded in the first three verses of chapter 12, the call is for Abraham to leave his country, his kinsmen, and his father's house. He is to go to a "country that I will show . . . " (12:1). There he will be made "into a great nation." This promise reflects God's blessing to Abraham but includes the promise of blessing to the entire world *through* Abraham.

This passage brings into focus a biblical theme that has appeared previously but in blurred form. The theme is that of God calling into being a people for himself. God will have a people. God's people will receive from God in order to share God with the world. As the theme develops, the members of this people have a tremendous struggle as they move toward a corporate identity. These struggles come primarily as a result of their resistance to doing God's will, of their unwillingness to acknowledge the sovereignty of God totally and completely.

Herein lies the importance of this passage. It spells out the action of God in calling out a people. It defines the nature of this people and their reason for existence. This people was to be the instrument of God's blessing to the world. This people was called into being through God's grace and was to be an instrument of that grace.

And the father of this people was to be Abraham. As such he is the prototype of the man of faith. We are introduced to him here in a rather casual fashion. We are not told of all his good qualities. We are not given a list of reasons to show why he should be chosen. He is simply described as one called by God. For the one who would be a person of faith in any age, it is important to see that the first characteristic described is that of obedience. The key statement is found in 12:4: "And so Abram set out *as the Lord had bidden him*" (author's emphasis).

A phrase is added here that also appears in 13:1. It is "and Lot went with him." Abraham's nephew Lot traveled with the man of faith. Just as we can get from Abraham a picture of what it is to be human and a person of faith, so we can get from Lot one picture of what it is to be human and *other than* a person of faith. The contrast underscores the lesson. As Lot's life-style develops, as his values are revealed, the dimensions of faith are more clearly delineated. No single event is decisive, but over a period of many years and in the description of succeeding choices, the picture becomes quite clear. When we read Genesis, we find much to learn from the life of Lot. Later in our story we will look more closely at these lessons.

But it is Abraham who occupies the center stage. He is given real estate by divine dispensation. The land is to be his and his descendants', according to 12:7. But the passage that follows becomes particularly important. It reads:

> So Abram built an altar there to the Lord who had appeared to him. Thence he went on to the hill-country east of Bethel and pitched his tent between Bethel on

the west and Ai on the east. There he built an altar to
the LORD and invoked the LORD by name" (12:7b-8).

More important than the gift of the land is the Giver. The
issue of most significance is the nature of the relationship
between Abraham and God. Wherever Abraham went, he
built an altar. Further, it was at the place of the second altar
that Abraham ". . . invoked the LORD by name" (12:8b).

Here, as in much of the Bible, the emphasis is upon relating and relationships. Abraham had a special relationship
to God; this was demonstrated by the fact that he knew him
"by name." It was a relationship of intimacy, of closeness.
God had revealed himself and made himself known to Abraham. Yet, in this self-revelation there was no blurring of the
distinction between the two. Abraham saw God as God,
built an altar, and worshiped him. Abraham did not aspire
to be like God but only to fulfill his created potential and
to discover the highest form of relationship possible between himself and his Creator.

If the full individuality of God was revealed and maintained, so was that of Abraham. In the relationship with God
he was not swallowed up. He was not freed from the necessity of making decisions. What follows the statement of
his call and his response makes abundantly clear that his
humanity was in no way affected. He was faced with decisions regarding his social environment. In the first decision
his freedom to choose is evident in that he made the wrong
choice. In the second, his was the right choice, but both
choices were his to make. God was present in both but did
not interfere with Abraham's growth as a person. God was
there to protect; he was there to redeem the situation when
mistakes were made.

The first of these incidents is a particularly difficult one
for modern sensitivities. A primitive culture and values are
reflected which we would not find acceptable today. The
incident smacks of sexism and exploitation of the worst sort.
It reveals Abraham's weakness and a strange lack of trust
for a person of faith. It concerns Abraham's wife Sarah and
his willingness to place her in Pharaoh's harem to preserve

his own life. Verses ten through twenty of chapter 12 are unlikely candidates for sermon texts, but they do give insight into God's manner of relating. Finding himself in alien surroundings and threatening circumstances, Abraham allowed Sarah to be added to the king's harem, saying that she was his sister. God then intervened to let the king know the true nature of Sarah's relationship to Abraham, and she was restored to Abraham's household.

An obvious reason for the inclusion of this ugly little story is to show that God will protect the purity of the line in order to establish his people. He moved to prevent any sexual impurity in Sarah. When she produced the heir according to God's announcement, there was no question of parentage.

Another reason concerns Abraham's growth as a person of faith. He was obedient to the call of God, demonstrating his trust in God. Then Abraham showed himself to have unenlightened areas of life. There were some areas in his life in which fear reigned and not God. God brought light to these areas, and, as a result, Abraham could grow in his awareness of how far God could be trusted.

That this area of trust had grown is shown by the second incident. Abraham's economic growth created some problems in his relationship with Lot. It seemed advisable that they separate. On this occasion Abraham gave Lot first choice. Lot's choice was immediate and self-centered.

> Lot looked up and saw how well-watered the whole Plain of the Jordan was; all the way to Zoar it was like the Garden of the LORD, like the land of Egypt. . . . So Lot chose all the Plain of the Jordan and took the road on the east side (13:10-12).

Abraham could accept the land of lesser value, trusting in God's promise to bless him.

Thus we are introduced to the man of faith. He was not perfect by any means, but he emerges as a growing person, growing in an awareness of the depth to which God can be trusted. Unlike our too frequent depictions of the religious person, here is no emphasis upon perfection. Abraham's claim to fame is his willing obedience and capacity to grow. If one would be a person of faith today, the requirements are the same: one should act in obedient response to what revelation one has received and should stay open to further revelation and greater understanding.

Questions for Reflection

1. On a map in a Bible atlas, note the journey of Terah from Ur to Haran and Abraham's journey to Bethel. To what kind of journey in today's world could you compare this in terms of the depth of trust required?

2. At what points in your life have you felt the call to live by faith?

3. In what areas of your life do you find the faith choice more difficult than others? Identify some areas of insecurity in your life.

4. The cultural situation in which Abraham could gain safety by calling Sarah his sister seems quite remote from our time. However, the lack of faith evident here may be present in all of us. In what ways could the safety of family members be compromised because of a person's lack of faith?

5. With God's action and attitude toward Cain, Noah, and Abraham, one can begin to see the thread of God's grace that runs throughout the biblical revelation. In what way does the knowledge of God's grace allow you the freedom to be an authentic person?

6. Abraham chose to let Lot go his own way; he chose not to control him or to be his keeper. On what occasions have you allowed family members to make their own mistakes? Under what circumstances would you find that very difficult to do?

5

"Behind Every Great Man. . . ."

Genesis 16:1–18:15; 21:1-21

S omeone has said that behind every great man there is a woman. The implication is that a great man may appear to be self-sufficient but that in the background there will be a supporting cast of one significant woman. I suspect that in addition to being interesting folklore, this thought might support our thesis concerning completeness in male and female. In Abraham's case we concede his greatness, and we don't have far to look for the woman. Her influence was considerable, and her importance in the story should never be minimized.

The story of Sarah is remarkable indeed. Coming, as it does, out of a culture that treated women as inferior, it is nothing short of amazing. In occasional lapses Abraham regarded Sarah as property and sent her off to the king's harem, but the total narrative pictures her as an individual of equal importance to Abraham. Her individuality was never lost, and she emerges as a person of faith in her own right.

Sarah's part in the drama begins to take shape in chapter 16. It is evident that she was not simply a passive instrument by which the call to Abraham was to be fulfilled. She was one who was involved—even to taking leadership. When no heir appeared after several years, she suggested that Abraham use her slave girl, Hagar, to produce the child through whom God would bless the world. The results of this suggestion were sad but very revealing from a human point of view. They also led to rather important lessons regarding faith.

Ishmael was born of the union of Abraham and Hagar. Apparently, even before delivery of the child, the jealousy of Sarah (or Hagar's arrogance, or both) caused serious domestic strife. Sarah regreted her suggestion and began to treat pregnant Hagar poorly. Hagar ran away, but divine intervention caused her return and Ishmael was born.

Already certain characteristics of Sarah are visible. She was dedicated to helping her husband fulfill his destiny. She was a person very much in touch with her own feelings. She leaned toward impulsiveness. She had leadership qualities and was inclined to be aggressive and forceful. But in her relationship to God she had considerable growing to do. She believed God but didn't believe he could carry out his promises without outside assistance. She was impatient, reading the situation entirely from her limited human perspective. In short, she believed but needed help for her unbelief.

Chapter 17 begins with a renewal of the promise of God to Abraham. The covenant was spelled out in more detail. Circumcision was added as a symbolic requirement for the males belonging to the covenant people. This addition pointed to a male-dominated people, but a further statement softened that. It concerned Sarah. She was named as co-creator with Abraham (see verses 15 and 16). From this point on, there was no question as to the significance of her role.

With the clarification of Sarah's role there came a response that certainly deserves more publicity. Abraham found God's statement that Sarah would bear a son beyond belief; he found it laughable. He could not believe that God could work the kind of miracle that would allow for conception in a woman beyond menopause. According to the record (vv. 17-18), he actually laughed at the suggestion and offered a counter proposal that would utilize Ishmael to continue the line. However, not only did God insist on Sarah being the one to bear Abraham a son, but God added another instruction, which makes this, for me, one of the delightful passages of the Bible. Abraham was told to name his son "Isaac," which means "he laughed." God had heard Abraham's laugh and did not directly rebuke him; God simply insisted on having the last laugh!

Now Sarah is officially a member of the team, and we meet her again in the events of Chapter 18. Heavenly visitors came to Abraham's tent. He treated them hospitably, offering them a good meal. The visitors reiterated the promise of parentage for Abraham and Sarah. This time it was Sarah, eavesdropping, who laughed. Later, when asked about her laughter, she denied it, though her denial was not accepted. Interestingly enough, there is no indication of punishment or rebuke for her laughter or her denial. It is just a part of the record that doubt does not prevent the work of God in the world, even when the doubt exists in God's primary servants.

Sarah appears with a major part in the drama once more in chapter 21. Here is the account of the birth of Isaac. In view of the emphasis on laughter recorded in previous chapters, we are not surprised at Sarah's announcement at Isaac's birth. According to verse 6, she said, "God has given me good reason to laugh, and everybody who hears will laugh with me." The lesson here seems significant. It would appear that when God has the last laugh, there is laughter enough to go around for everyone.

So behind Abraham there was a woman. Not only was she *behind* him but, in spite of the cultural conditioning against it, she was seen to be *with* him, by choice as well as by chance. Sarah's individuality was always evident. She owned her own feelings—for good or ill. Hers was a growing faith—growing through doubt and personal weakness. To those of any age who would be fully human, she provides a significant example.

Questions for Reflection

1. In reading about the laughter of Abraham and Sarah, can you see any implications for your relationship to God? How honest and personally authentic are you in your prayer experience?

2. When doubt threatens your relationship to God, to whom can you turn to talk it out? What happens if you attempt to ignore the doubt?

3. How do you recognize in yourself the tendency to take charge and run ahead of God? How can you keep your concern and commitment without running ahead of God?

4. When Hagar was pregnant and Sarah was not, the circumstances made it easy for Hagar to lord it over Sarah. Have you had experiences in your own life that influence your thinking about Hagar and Sarah?

6

Enough to Save a City

Genesis 19

Of the three people (Abraham, Sarah, and Lot) who originally responded to the call of God, two remain on the pilgrimage. Abraham and Sarah now share equally as the instruments through which the people of God will emerge. Both are committed to God's purpose; each remains an individual in the response of faith. Together they have experienced community. Lot remains related to them, but that relationship is tenuous indeed. By choice he has "pitched his tents near Sodom" (13:12-13), indicating that that city will now be the source of community for him. He is attracted to and affected by that culture.

Perhaps it would have been tactful simply to draw the curtain on Lot at that point. His further adventures are not pretty, and they are not really a part of the calling into being of God's people. They do, however, reveal something of the nature of the people of Sodom—particularly the nature of their relationship to those outside the community. Lot's story also illustrates the danger of choosing the wrong city in which to dwell.

Sodom and Gomorrah are two names that have become synonymous with evil in the highest (or lowest?) degree.

They also are reminders of judgment and the ultimate destruction of evil. Very little in the narrative concerning them is palatable. We can only approach the passages cautiously.

As we focus our attention on the story, the first thing we see is the attitude of Abraham toward his kinsman and the city of Sodom. Apprised of the impending doom, he immediately entered into dialogue with God. He did his best to find some way by which the city could be saved. In an experience of bargaining that would do justice to a Middle Eastern bazaar, he sought to find the irreducible minimum of good people that would insure the city's salvation. Beginning with fifty, he worked his way down to ten. If even ten good people could be found, God would withhold judgment.

This account tells us much about the relationship of Abraham to God. This is Old Testament prayer at its best. It shows Abraham's deep concern for people and his willingness to intercede before God for them. The audacity of this man of faith is evident. Also, his values are evident. He knows the wickedness of the city of Sodom, and yet he still wants to stay God's judgment of it. For even a very small number of the population the city could be saved. This story points to a value system that sees importance in just one sheep out of a flock of a hundred.

But Abraham's concern went for naught. Apparently the ten couldn't be found. Our attention is turned to Lot and the judgment that came. Lot was saved from the destruction but at a terrible cost. His wife died because of her unwillingness to flee without looking back. Was the attraction of that culture just too much, or was she unable to trust that a new life could be built? At any rate, Lot found himself with a shattered home and terribly broken family.

Sometimes, as I read this, I wonder why Abraham stopped at ten good people. Why didn't he go on with the bargaining till he could convince God to save the city for only Lot's sake? On the other hand, why couldn't Lot see the impending doom and intercede for the city himself?

I am not sure of the answers to these questions, but I am

convinced that raising them is important. The person of faith has found himself or herself close to doomed cities in many ages. His or her attitude has always been one of deep concern; his or her effort will always be put forth for the city's salvation. (Unless, of course, the person's name is Jonah; then he is in line for the rebuke of God.) But how much of a saving remnant will it take?

Perhaps Lot can teach us some lessons. By pitching his tent toward Sodom, he was identifying with that culture. Could there be a warning in this against identification with any given culture? I suspect that this is part of the message. If a person can accept the status quo so easily, he or she may destroy any redemptive capabilities he or she may have.

But let's look further. A cultural feature of Sodom was homosexuality. Lot had seen the extent to which this had spread. In Genesis 19:4, there is a statement that the men of Sodom demanded that Lot turn over his male visitors for sexual purposes: ". . . the men of Sodom, both young and old, surrounded the house—everyone without exception." "Everyone without exception" would indicate rather widespread acceptance of this practice. It would appear that homosexuality was a way of life for Sodom.

This could make it easy for us to attack the immorality of homosexual activity. I see something other than that. Lot had identified with a city whose inhabitants could no longer cope with differences creatively. God created individuals as male or female. "Male" and "female" refer to human differences. When these differences are observed and celebrated, each can be fulfilled in the other. This is the first step toward establishing a creative community. The issue is not the sexual practice per se but the fact that a large segment of humanity was being denied the opportunity for fulfillment. Women were ignored and excluded from the social scene. Only men counted.

History emphasizes the lesson that surfaces here. A community that destroys, exploits, discriminates against, or in any way denies personhood to a segment of its members is under the judgment of God. Whether destruction comes through a rain of fire from heaven or by slow erosion from within is not as important as recognition of the inevitability of that judgment. To build community is to allow for individuality and basic human differences. In Sodom, individuality had been lost and only mob action remained. It was time for divine intervention!

As terrible as this narrative is, as much as we might like to excise it from our holy book, it has a significance for the contemporary reader that should not be missed. Lot apparently did not participate fully in the life and culture of Sodom, but neither did he clearly identify himself with another culture or people. His tacit acceptance of the status quo placed him in a precarious position. Rather than being a part of a saving remnant, he drifted into a state of helplessness. He couldn't be what he might have been—enough to save a city.

Questions for Reflection

1. Are there any criteria for determining when a person is coming under the influence of a particular culture? Compare Noah with Lot.

2. How does one recognize a dying culture? What evidence will there be that a group of people is under the judgment of God?

3. How would you recognize Lot's choices if they were to appear to you in this age? To what extent are you entangled in your culture? To what extent can you associate with your neighbors while still living by your own principles?

4. Beyond simply remaining free of sins of the "city" in which you dwell, how can you become an influence in its salvation?

7

Tests of Faith

Genesis 20–22

Chapter 20 is one passage that could probably be eliminated from the Bible with no loss of meaning. The contents repeat an incident from chapter 12. It adds little new to the unfolding drama of the people of God, and it certainly is not pleasant reading. Still, it does add emphasis to what we have already learned. It serves to underscore the fact that God wills to have a people and is responsible for bringing that people into being through the instruments he has chosen.

Once again Abraham, as the man of faith, found himself being tested. The circumstances resulted from his social and political environment. Seeing himself surrounded by hostile forces, he became frightened. His choice then was to place himself under God's protective care or to negotiate for his own safety apart from God. He chose the latter method and allowed Sarah to become a member of Abimelech's harem.

There was a rather strange result in all of this. Abraham succeeded, even while he was failing the test of faith. God oversaw the negotiation and exposed it as false. Not only was the sexual purity of Sarah maintained but Abraham's political situation was strengthened. This story shows us that God uses the weakness of human beings and still achieves his purpose.

Significantly, it was right after this test that Sarah conceived. This incident appears to have been one more assurance that the establishment of a Chosen People was God's work and that it was to be accomplished through Abraham. The line of God's people would remain pure.

But in the next recorded event we learn that God's Chosen People suffered from such sins as jealousy. After the birth of Isaac, Sarah became very conscious of the presence of Hagar and Ishmael. Just what the event was that triggered her anger is not clear. But angry she was, and she ordered Abraham to remove the two from the family.

In what follows we have further insight into the character of Abraham. Like most humans he was a strange mixture of strength and weakness, toughness and softness. He had a great wish to be fair and a need to avoid difficult decisions. We may see inconsistency in the fact that he could use Sarah to protect himself from pagan kings and yet yielded to her on the domestic scene. However, this simply shows him to be a man with a normal complement of ambivalences and anxieties.

What is demonstrated in this account is God's role, and it is interesting, to say the least. God did not intervene in the domestic strife but allowed Abraham to do what he felt had to be done. Because God expended so much effort to keep the line pure and to insure that Abraham and Sarah shared in it, we might expect that God would ignore the plight of Hagar and Ishmael. However, he did not; indeed, God protected them and promised that Ishmael would be the father of a great people as well. Though God was choosing a special people, this fact did not eliminate a concern for all of humanity.

So Abraham experienced tests and struggles from his social and political environment. He experienced the threat of domestic strife. In each instance God entered the picture to resolve the situation.

Then Abraham faced the really big test: God's order to Abraham to sacrifice his son Isaac. Because many centuries have elapsed since then and our culture is very different, it is difficult for us to enter into this story. It seems shocking beyond words and terribly gross. In spite of the difficulties involved, some significant lessons emerge and the story cannot be ignored.

The first of these lessons is obedience. A person of faith must live by the principle of obedience. Abraham was obedient when he first responded to God's call. He had to reaffirm his decision to be obedient in the toughest decision a father could face. God told him to sacrifice this son of his old age, to put to death this long-awaited heir.

If it doesn't mean anything else, this story speaks of humanity's priorities. The relationship to God comes first. God is sovereign, and that sovereignty must be the first principle in the establishment of his people. He will call them into being; he will establish their purpose; he will rule. Early in the history of God's people this principle was affirmed in perhaps the most dramatic way possible.

Genesis 22 presents one of the truly great challenges of the entire Bible. At first glance the passage seems painfully out of character for the God we see revealed elsewhere. Yet it prepares us for other difficult passages, such as Jesus' words in Luke 14:26:

'If anyone comes to me and does not hate his father and mother, wife and children, brothers and sisters, even his own life, he cannot be a disciple of mine.'

Certainly, too, it is preparation for the words in Matthew 6:24:

'No servant can be the slave of two masters; for either he will hate the first and love the second, or he will be devoted to the first and think nothing of the second. You cannot serve God and Money.'

So the chapter begins with these words: "The time came when God put Abraham to the test." The nature of the test concerns Isaac and the order to:

'Take your son Isaac, your only son, whom you love, and go to the land of Moriah. There you shall offer him as a sacrifice on one of the hills which I will show you' (22:2).

God is saying rather clearly that he is the giver of life and that he retains control over it. But is that all that is being said?

We are, of course, relieved by the outcome. Isaac was not sacrificed in a literal sense, but in Abraham's willingness and preparation for the sacrifice, we can believe that the relationship between father and son was changed. It is here that we find another biblical truth coming to the surface of the biblical record. In the strongest way possible we are told that any relationship that would dim the awareness of the sovereignty of God is a dangerous one. It is not that God needed to prove his sovereignty for his own sake but that Abraham needed an experience to regain perspective. Once Abraham had a son, he felt complete. In that son his name and family line was preserved. He was tempted to focus all of his attention upon that son. It would have been easy for Abraham to forget that Isaac was a gift and, therefore, easy for him to forget the source of the gift. In loving Isaac too much, he was in danger of losing the meaning of love. Further, Abraham needed to experience again the basic love and trust that would give meaning to all other loves.

It was a harsh and hard lesson but even great men of faith need to learn this way. Abraham's trust was deep enough to allow him to come through this test. When he could give up that which was most dear to him, he was then in a position to receive all things. Here again is that strange paradox that keeps emerging in the Bible: we only get by giving. We can only hold those things that are given away.

This is a lesson of such fundamental importance that we really need a story like this to get our attention. In an age that has so terribly confused possession with love, we need to hear God speak through this event. Many, many parents have "loved" their children right into destruction. Unable to release them, these parents, clutching and grabbing, have choked the life out of their children. Love always has its roots in freedom. To give freedom to one in whom our affection and emotions are heavily invested demands trust to an intense degree. Parents throughout the ages have discovered the importance of releasing their children into the hands of God. Attempts to usurp God's place, to act as God to their children, have been disastrous. It is to the extent that we trust God, that we are persons of faith, that the climate of freedom can be present to promote the growth of love.

Questions for Reflection

1. God seems to have intervened in the lives of Abraham and Sarah "to keep the line pure." How would you interpret this thought? What is being kept pure—the family line, the blood type, the race, or the obedient relationship with God?

2. Put yourself in Abraham's shoes. What would you be thinking and feeling as you made the three-day journey to sacrifice your son?

3. Can you think of any families in your surrounding community where the parents' intense "love" for their children actually destroyed the children? Can you think of examples when parents sacrificed their children on an altar of their own need?

4. How would you distinguish the point at which a person's attraction for and attachment to another human become possessive and therefore destructive?

5. The first of the Ten Commandments is "You shall have no other god to set against me." In what ways is this commandment designed to protect humanity?

8

From Son to Patriarch

Genesis 23–24

W e meet Isaac when his father was put to the test. In that dramatic moment Isaac played a passive role. He did inquire concerning the sacrifice, but when it became apparent that he was to be the sacrifice there is no record of any resistance on his part. Isaac's reaction when he was released is not mentioned. Perhaps it would be safe to say that this set the tone for Isaac's life. Of all the patriarchs, he showed the least aggressiveness. This quietness could reflect the trust in God that Isaac learned in this experience.

But before Isaac could take over as leader of the clan, he had some final business with Abraham. Chapter 23 contains the account of the burial of Sarah. The experience is significant because it demonstrated Abraham's determination to be independent of the culture around him. The growth in trust manifested here reflects the lessons learned in Lot's experience. Abraham refused to be indebted even for a burial plot. Though he was offered one free, he payed the full going rate.

Chapter 24 is the transition from focusing on Abraham to focusing on Isaac. Abraham recognized his approaching death and prepared Isaac for leadership by finding him a suitable bride. He did not want a bride from the surrounding alien tribes but one who was part of his own tribe and shared the family religious tradition. Thus he sent a servant to procure one.

This unnamed servant not only did his job well but showed himself to be a person of considerable ability. He also showed the religious influence from Abraham's household and some uncommon common sense. Seeking divine guidance, he set up a sign for determining God's selection. The sign was one that would indicate the girl to be generous and cooperative. When Rebecca showed the sign, he very tactfully proceeded with the negotiations. Because he used such a devout and careful approach, we are not surprised that he was successful.

The process introduced Rebecca and pointed to her as a worthy successor to Sarah in the line of patriarchs' wives. She is described as beautiful and generous. She also demonstrated at this early stage that she would be a person in her own right. Though quite young (24:59 mentions that a nurse was sent with her), she was still consulted by her father and her older brother, Laban, before she made the return journey with Abraham's servant.

Speaking of Laban, he played a fairly important role later on. There are some early, clear indications of his character. Verse 30 of chapter 24 gives us the first clue: ". . . When he saw the nose-ring, and also the bracelets on his sister's wrists . . . ." This gives us the hint that material display affected him. The servant apparently recognized that fact and opened his negotiations with an account of his master's wealth. Laban doesn't come through as very attractive. Later experience will confirm the first impression.

Knowing that his son had a suitable wife, Abraham could depart in peace. Chapter 25 is the account of his last days, particularly of his efforts to insure that there would be one clearly defined line of promise through Isaac. Though Abraham had had other children by a second wife and by concubines, these had been dismissed "to a land of the east, out of his son Isaac's way." Ishmael's descendants were named but primarily so that that line could be tidied up before Abraham concentrated on Isaac.

As a patriarch, Isaac was somewhat undistinguished. He exhibited the same weak conduct that his father had and attempted to pass his wife off as his sister. Again God intervened so that no evil came of it. In other experiences he appeared rather passive. For instance, his servants dug a series of wells that were taken over by local tribesmen. Isaac simply named each one and moved on. Though he was wealthy and powerful, he did not contend for any of the wells. He finally ended up with one named Rehoboth, meaning "plenty of room."

Perhaps Isaac's passive nature is a lesson in itself. He was not the pioneer that Abraham was when he left his country and kinsmen in response to God's call. Isaac did not exhibit the aggressiveness of Jacob, nor did he have to go through the agonizing experience of wrestling all night as Jacob did. Still he maintained the line of God's people. In chapter 26 God renews his promise to multiply Isaac's descendants. With that revelation Isaac "built an altar there and invoked the LORD by name." Isaac now knew God. Up till now God has been referred to as the "God of Abraham." From this point on he will be known as the "God of Abraham and the God of Isaac." What God is looking for is not someone willing to accomplish great things for him, but someone willing to open oneself to a knowledge of him and be a witness to God's presence in the world. No special personality trait is more desirable than another. An open responsiveness to the call of God is the basic concern.

Questions for Reflection

1. Can you recognize ways in which you can become indebted to your surrounding culture that would lead to destructiveness in your relationship to God?

2. The account of Isaac and the controversy over the wells

raises the question "When should you stand up and fight and when should you back away?" If there is no clear-cut answer, how do we live with the tension of that kind of choice?

3. If you were to list certain criteria for the person you would consider marrying, what would you include on the list?

4. As you consider Isaac's relationship to God, think of your own faith pilgrimage. At what point in your life could you honestly say, "My God," rather than "my parents' God" or "my friend's God"?

9

Pottage, a Hard Pillow, and Long Nights

Genesis 25:19–33:11

I f Isaac comes off a bit colorless, that is not the problem with his son Jacob. From the moment of his birth, Jacob was a strong and willful character who knew what he wanted and worked to get it. Though not the logical successor to Isaac in the line of God's people (Esau was born first), he assumed that role. We learn how this happened and get some very significant lessons about God's relationship to humanity in the process. It is my opinion that, with the exception of King David, no other Old Testament character is as interesting to study, carries as much dramatic potential, or can teach us as much about ourselves as can Jacob.

Though the story of Jacob appears simple, there is an element in it that is very disturbing. It is part of a biblical theme that has invited confusion and controversy to a tremendous degree. We call it predestination; there is evidence that God *predestined* Jacob to his special role. This evidence raises questions for which there are no definitive answers. Why did God choose Jacob? Why did God choose a peculiar people for himself? Is it right for God to have favorites?

As we wrestle with these questions, factors can be identified that give us partial answers. God is and will be involved in much of the world's action at the initiating stage. He refuses to be treated as a last resort—someone dragged into the drama to untangle a hopelessly snarled plot. This underscores the fact of God's sovereignty. God remains free to act and doesn't just react.

This disturbing element of predestination appears in the record of the birth of the twins. Something occurred during her pregnancy that was upsetting to Rebecca. She sought God's word and was told she would bear two very different children. Each, in his own way, would be a leader. There would be continuing conflict between them. Contrary to cultural tradition, the elder would serve the younger. Though Jacob was not the first-born, God *chose* him to be the one through whom his line would descend.

Certainly the choice of Jacob is a strange one. Neither Esau nor Jacob appears to have been a likely candidate for sainthood. Esau was the rugged outdoorsman but rude and crude. He showed little or no sensitivity to spiritual values. Jacob was his mother's boy, preferring domestic chores. He did show an almost inordinate interest in spiritual things. Not only was he interested, but his determination to acquire religious leadership and family control knew no bounds. He did not let honesty block his way.

It was in this setting that the famous incident of the birthright occurred. Esau, by right of primogeniture, owned the birthright. The birthright did not offer any particular value in a property sense. The property was to be divided equally. However, it did make him the next in line to be the family priest. As such he would preside at religious festivals and exercise the most influence in tribal decisions.

Nearly everyone is aware of how Jacob got the birthright. Esau came in from a hunting trip, famished. Jacob offered him a mess of pottage (or lentils) in exchange for the birthright. The hungry Esau agreed.

Whether Esau actually scorned the birthright to this extent is not clear. His later anger would indicate that he might not have thought he was making a valid agreement. He might have thought the deal would not be complete until it was ratified by the father. A bowl of lentils may have started the transfer of the birthright from Esau to Jacob, but a considerable amount of trickery was needed to bring it off. Rebecca provided some of the brains, and there may even have been some collusion on Isaac's part. At any rate, by very devious means Jacob became the one through whom God's people would emerge. There seems little that would have recommended either the prosaic and insensitive Esau or the tricky and ambitious Jacob. For whatever reasons, God chose the younger brother, Jacob.

But after he had the birthright, life wasn't all ease and comfort for Jacob. He was afraid of what his terribly angry brother might do. Upon the advice of his mother, he left for her home country to find a wife and escape his brother's wrath.

One of the more familiar events of the Bible occurred on Jacob's first night away from home. Taking a stone for a pillow, he lay down for uneasy sleep. A strange dream reassured him. In the dream there was a ladder between earth and heaven, with angels ascending and descending it. Further, God stood next to him and re-confirmed the covenant that had come first to Abraham. Jacob was to be richly blest with lands and progeny. His descendants were to be an influence on all peoples.

Whatever else this dream might mean, it was awe-inspiring to Jacob and provided the encouragement for his continued pilgrimage. For us today it is more than just awe-inspiring. It is a source of hope beyond measure. Here was a scheming man in flight from a vengeful brother. We could expect little sympathy from God and might even expect judgment. Instead, God gave comfort and reassurance. In our own moments of fearful aloneness, God may come to us, and it won't necessarily be when we fully deserve it. God operates out of grace.

For Jacob the experience was extremely valuable because it prepared him for the testing that he was to experience shortly. Soon he was to meet and begin a relationship with his uncle Laban. This relationship began with warmth and tenderness. It proceeded through a period of competition and mutual exploitation. It ended in a treaty that reflected distrust and was simply an agreement to go separate ways.

The warmth and tenderness appear in chapter 29. Jacob met Rachel first. He found her tending a flock of sheep, and he assisted her in the task. Then he met his uncle and was welcomed as a kinsman. In a very brief span of time, physiological and emotional chemistry were at work and Jacob fell in love with Rachel. Negotiations were undertaken and Jacob agreed to work seven years in order to receive Rachel as his bride.

At the end of the seven-year period, Laban's true character was manifested. He tricked Jacob into marrying Leah, the elder sister. When Jacob questioned Laban about why he had tricked him into marrying Leah, Laban replied with some pious rationalizations and invoked a hitherto unmentioned custom of the land: The eldest daughter had to be married off first. Jacob was tricked, and there was no appeal to a higher court.

Jacob completed the week-long celebration after Laban had agreed that Rachel would also be his, in exchange for *another* seven years of labor. Apparently uncle and nephew were reconciled and all went well. But the tone of the relationship was established, and the entire family was soon caught up in a pattern of intrigue and trickery. Leah and Rachel became involved in a continuing power struggle in which Leah gained an early advantage. Though Jacob made no secret of his preference for Rachel, Leah was able to establish her feminine superiority by producing children while Rachel remained barren. Rachel countered by offering Jacob her slave girl. This union produced children and caused Leah to add her slave girl to the scene. Finally Rachel became pregnant and Joseph was born.

In relationship to the two women, Jacob is pictured somewhat as the innocent bystander who watched while they fought it out. In relationship to Laban the picture is different. Laban won round one when he palmed the elder daughter off on Jacob. From that point on Jacob didn't lose many battles, and he most certainly won the war. Though his methods might not be accepted as valid today, Jacob proved to be clever in amassing great wealth. He acquired most of Laban's flocks, as well as the enmity of Laban's sons. The sons could see what was happening and became fearful of ending up as paupers.

With the growing enmity between himself and Laban, Jacob thought once more of home. According to the biblical narrative (31:3), God put a favorable light on the issue with a reassuring statement that Jacob *should* return to his home country and God would journey with him. So Jacob brought his family together and planned the departure. Rachel and Leah were in wholehearted agreement with the plan and assisted in its implementation.

Indeed it was Rachel who added insult to injury as far as Laban was concerned. She stole his household gods. Given the reliance of that culture upon household gods for personal and family safety, it is not surprising that Laban gathered his forces and started after them. Here, too, we are given some insight into Rachel's character. She proved to be resourceful but as devious in her dealings with Laban as was Jacob. She placed the household gods under her saddle and then used menstruation as an excuse for not arising and allowing further search.

The parting between Laban and Jacob was peaceful but somewhat uneasy. A sacred pillar of stones was erected to stand between Laban and Jacob and each agreed not to cross the other's side. The pillar was named Mizpah, meaning "watch-tower." It became the setting for the well-known Mizpah benediction: "'May the LORD watch between you and me, when we are parted from each other's sight'" (31:49). It appears a bit strange that this benediction can be used so piously today when the original meaning was related to distrust. It meant, "Let the Lord keep his eye on you when

I can't see you for otherwise there is no telling what trickery you might be up to."

Jacob was approaching the climax of his life. As he advanced toward the Jabbok River, he became increasingly frightened of the impending confrontation with Esau. He appears to have genuinely desired the reconciliation with his brother. In his competition with Esau or with Laban, Jacob could fend for himself. However, as he approached Esau, he did not want competition; he desired reconciliation. Being a winner was not all that important. The capable and competent Jacob was faced with something that left him feeling helpless. He did not know how to be restored to a brother from whom he had become alienated.

What literally and physically took place that night at the Jabbok River cannot be fully known or understood. We can speculate that there were not two men literally engaged in a wrestling match. Quite likely only one physical body was present. Within that one body a tremendous struggle was taking place. The battleground was Jacob's inner being and, the prize would concern Jacob's future.

The results of the wrestling match are not clear either. What was quite clear was that Jacob was the winner; but he also may have been the loser. Something inside Jacob was defeated that night, but Jacob himself became a victor. He became a new person with a new name—Israel. The footnote or marginal note in some Bibles indicates that this new name described him as one whose primary concern would now be with his relationship with God. The struggle began because of the deep anxiety growing out of his alienation from his brother. To end that alienation something very significant had to happen in his relationship to God. That experience was an extremely important new beginning for Jacob.

To get this message in focus is to recognize a major theme of the entire Bible. How do we live in harmony with our brothers and sisters? How is it possible for such different personalities as Jacob and Esau to live in peace? How do we build community? A confrontation with God that reestablishes God's sovereignty in our personal experience ends the competition and self-seeking that destroy community.

The story of Jacob is a further emphasis upon the value of relationship. God created human beings with a strange capacity to choose. To jump from Jacob to the contemporary scene is not difficult. We know what it is to be caught in a competitive framework, and we have experienced the suspicion and anxiety generated by that competition. It is extremely important that we look as closely as possible at what Jacob found to be an escape from that scene. The answer is not found by participating in simple little religious exercises but by experiencing a struggle of deep magnitude. We acquire a name (an identity) as we are prepared to accept the role, in relationship to God, for which we have been created. Such a struggle may well go on throughout the entire night!

A feature of this story that has always intrigued me is the notation that Jacob continued on his journey from this place and experience, "limping because of his hip." The proud Jacob appears to have acquired some humility that would last throughout the remainder of his life. Certainly this was a strange experience, but the implications of it touch all of us. This long night of Jacob's was just too significant for any of us to ignore.

Questions for Reflection

1. What pattern can you find in God's election? What characteristics do you look for in God's chosen ones?

2. In the instances of sibling rivalry that you have seen, how did such rivalry affect the sense of family or community?

3. In moments of loneliness and fear how would you look and listen for the assurance that comes in the sentence "Surely I will be with you"?

4. As you read the account of Jacob and his wives, what problems would you anticipate among the sons?

5. As you read the life story of Jacob, what feelings toward him can you identify within yourself?

6. In your own wrestling with a problem of conscience and/or of broken relationships, what did you lose and what did you gain from the struggle?

10

Pride and Providential Care

Genesis 34–41

Jacob struggled all night and found a new identity. Reconciled with God, he was to be reconciled also with his brother Esau. All would now be peaceful and calm in his life. He could settle into a life of a prosperous country gentleman.

Wrong.

Though the experience at the Jabbok was redemptive, bringing Jacob into a restored relationship with God and Esau, it did not automatically free him from the consequences of previous actions and attitudes. We would expect that a family that began in deception and lived its early history in competition and suspicion would have a stormy existence. This proved to be painfully true in the experience of Jacob's family.

The fact that trouble is in store for the family is clearly seen in the ugly incident recorded in chapter 34. Dinah, Jacob's daughter, became involved in the social life of the neighboring people. This resulted in a sexual relationship with one of the young men of that tribe. The culprit was the son of a local prince, a member of a good family. After the seduction (or rape—the wording is not clear), the young man professed his love for Dinah and asked for her hand in marriage. Her angry brothers, led by Simeon and Levi, set a trap for the men of the neighboring community and murdered them.

Interpreting such a story is not easy. Some of the significance is found in the character of Jacob's sons. They showed considerable family loyalty, but they also showed a vicious vindictiveness and an impulsiveness not very attractive in those who would be part of the people of God.

Jacob's interpretation was that this vengeful and impulsive act reflected a lack of faith in God. Since he also saw it as inviting further revenge by kinsmen of the slain men, he became extremely frightened. His response to the fear was to order the destruction of any idolatrous material and lead the family in a return to Bethel for a renewal of the entire family's relationship to God. The visit to Bethel restored Jacob's faith and God again promised great blessings through his heirs.

In spite of the restoration of Jacob's relationship to God and renewal of the promise of future blessing, Jacob's family found itself suffering more tragedy. Shortly after leaving Bethel, Rachel died while giving birth to Benjamin. During the mourning period an event occurred that got very brief notice but portrays more family sickness. The eldest son, Reuben, had intercourse with one of his father's concubines, and the matter was brought to his father's attention. The Scriptures say nothing further about the incident, but here is a glimpse into the serious destructive competition present within the family.

In chapter 37 the family problems appear openly and in detail. Pride and competition among the brothers resulted in more pain for Jacob. One brother was the focal point for the problems, and this one brother has become a model for God's providential care. Certain elements, if not all of the story, are very well known to all who have had any church school experience at all. However, the total story needs to be told to us if we are to get the full impact of Joseph's personality.

Joseph was the son of Jacob's favorite wife. He enjoyed special privileges and was arrogant toward his brothers. Not only did Joseph dream dreams in which he was exercising domination over his brothers, but compulsively he related those dreams to his brothers. Small wonder that the brothers developed a resentment toward him!

The resentment reached a point of climax one day when Joseph visited his brothers, who were out in the field with the flocks. Wearing his famous coat of many colors, Joseph approached the brothers to find their jealousy fully inflamed. At first the brothers planned to kill him, but one brother, Judah, convinced the others that it would be better to sell him into slavery. Placed in a pit until the sale could be accomplished, Joseph was released by some Midianite merchants who sold him to some Ishmaelites traveling in a caravan to Egypt. Thus Joseph's life was spared, but he was separated from his family.

If God's providential care was apparent in this act of preservation, it becomes even more obvious in the events in Egypt. Beginning as a slave, Joseph traveled a path that took him to a position of nearly absolute control in the political structure of Egypt. The path was not at all smooth, and Joseph had to overcome some rather frightening obstacles along the way.

In the Genesis account, the sojourn of Joseph in Egypt does not occur immediately after his sale into slavery. Chapter 38 is a break from Joseph's story and is one of those biblical passages that tends to be an embarrassment. The continuity of the Joseph story is destroyed by the insertion of this material, and the material itself is difficult to interpret and harsh on human sensitivities. Still, chapter 38 is in Genesis, and we shouldn't or can't ignore it.

So leaving Joseph for a brief time, let's focus our attention on his brother Judah. Among other problems in Judah's family was the tendency of the sons to die before they produced heirs. This made for particular difficulties for the daughters-in-law. Without children, the daughters-in-law were left in a very vulnerable situation in the family structure. Judah asked one such widow, Tamar by name, to wait until a third son matured. He promised that then she could marry the third son. When Judah forgot that promise, Tamar jolted him back to it by a coarse strategem that does little to enhance the image of either.

Why such a story as this gained status enough to be included in the canon is not clear. The fact that the hero (?) of the story is Judah, who became the one through whom the line of God's people was to run, only adds to the confusion. Perhaps it is a reminder that God will not wait until he has only perfect instruments through whom to work. He simply asks that we be pliable and open to doing his will and that we grow in our understanding of that will.

Meanwhile, back in Egypt, Joseph was serving a new owner. Conducting himself admirably, Joseph moved up the social scale to become personal servant to his master. Then followed a series of events that made Joseph look a bit like a character in a television soap opera. Threatened and framed by a wanton woman, forgotten by colleagues whom he befriended, he still kept the faith. When Pharaoh needed a wise man to interpret his strange dreams, Joseph was ready. Not only did Joseph survive his inauspicious beginning in a strange land, but he moved to a place of great prominence.

That the story of Joseph is a difficult one to assimilate into our modern life was impressed upon me by an experience in a church I was serving as pastor. We were doing an in-depth study of the Joseph narrative. In small groups we were exploring the meaning of the story and translating that into our current setting by role-playing various situations. We had no difficulty seeing family dysfunction and family disintegration. Some problems were felt by those considering God's providential care. However, those trying to picture and act out family restoration experienced total failure. All attempts to bring the account of Joseph's reconciliation into the modern scene ended in failure. This may say something about that particular congregation, but I suspect it says something also about the difficulty we have in understanding the nature of forgiveness. That part of Joseph's life needs its own treatment.

Questions for Reflection

1. What insights about maintaining healthy family relationships have you gained from the account of Joseph and his brothers?

2. Compare Joseph's arrogance as a youth with his cautious approach to the reconciliation with his brothers.

3. What would you do if you found a brother or a sister or a friend to be a threat to some aspect of your values? What if you found yourself becoming a threat to the values of someone else?

4. How would you outline a role-playing situation that would depict the providence of God in a modern setting?

5. How would you outline a role-playing situation that would depict forgiveness and reconciliation in a modern family?

11

Painful Repentance and Tears of Joy

Genesis 42–45

The patterns of relationship within the family of Jacob are hardly subtle. Competition and struggle for recognition are clearly evident. Jacob demonstrated intense competitive spirit in his struggle with Esau and in his actions with his father-in-law. Rachel and Leah competed with each other in ways that seem to us to be crass and crude. We would expect to see competition among the children, and we certainly do.

As we have seen, Joseph was the early target for the other brothers. Being favored by the father gave him a vulnerable place in the competitive structure. Since he was the primary threat, the brothers could cooperate against him. They attempted to force him out of the family. There is no evidence that the removal of Joseph reduced competition among the brothers. It did, however, result in an incomplete family and in terrible pain for the father.

In varying degrees, family disintegration experienced by Jacob's family is being repeated regularly in our own culture. We don't see very many brothers being thrown into pits to be sold later into slavery, but we see many being driven from their families. We see many brokenhearted parents and many broken and incomplete families. Once it is broken by arrogance, jealousy, competition, and greed, is it possible for that family to be reunited? The account of Joseph and his brothers provides some hope.

To understand the elements in family reconciliation we need a fairly complete understanding of the events in the Joseph story. Though Joseph was driven out of the family, he refused to yield to despair. He chose to live by principle no matter how threatened he was by immediate circumstances. This is most clearly demonstrated by his experience with Potiphar's wife but is a factor in all subsequent events as well. Though to overemphasize Joseph's integrity would perhaps be wrong, it does need to be mentioned. I suspect that any family reconciliation must begin with one wronged member choosing to ignore personal pain and choosing to maintain commitment to the family.

Another element in the family experience was that of crisis brought on by a famine. Because of the crisis, the brothers of Joseph were forced to abandon a quiet routine existence and travel to Egypt. Through this visit they encountered Joseph and ultimately reconciled with him.

Though painful to admit, crisis may have to be present for family members to be reconciled to one another. It would appear that, left to our own devices, most of us would prefer lives of quiet desperation to experiencing the painful aspects involved in the forgiveness experience.

The unity of Jacob's family was shattered by the violence done to Joseph. The crisis of famine forced the brothers to visit Egypt. Upon arriving in Egypt, they encountered the brother whom they had wronged. What happens in this kind of encounter becomes important to our understanding of the process of forgiveness. Chapter 42 begins the record of the climactic events of the Joseph story.

Jacob sent ten of the brothers to Egypt. Showing that he still suffered from the loss of Joseph, he kept Benjamin with him in the family home. Here is evidence that the family's feeling of disunity remained.

Arriving in Egypt, the brothers encountered Joseph, but

they did not recognize him. In the initial stages of negotiation Joseph treated them with considerable harshness, accusing them of being spies. In their defensiveness they revealed facts about the family, and so Joseph learned of Benjamin and his father. Maintaining a posture of toughness, Joseph demanded that the brothers produce Benjamin or be held guilty as charged. In making his accusations and demands, Joseph used an interpreter, which further concealed his identity from his brothers.

Concealing his identity was only the first trick Joseph played on the brothers. The second consisted of keeping his brother Simeon as a hostage even while he planned to return the money they had paid by hiding it in their sacks of grain. This trick left the entire family terribly upset and confused. Only the threat of starvation induced Jacob to allow the brothers to return with Benjamin as Joseph had demanded.

When they arrived in Egypt with Benjamin, the brothers were put through a rather strange ordeal by Joseph. First, Joseph arranged for them to eat with him. Hearing of this, the brothers became very frightened, suspecting some kind of trap. Speaking to one of Joseph's attendants, they carefully explained that they had found the silver in the grain sacks, and they tried to get out of going to the meal. Joseph's steward attempted to put their minds at ease by explaining that it was their God who had hidden the treasure in their sacks (43:23).

Hardly reassured by the steward's comment, the brothers entered Joseph's quarters. As they were seated for the meal, they discovered that Joseph had arranged the seating according to the brother's ages. Joseph showed preferential treatment to Benjamin, but whether this was further puzzlement to the brothers is not known.

By the time the brothers were ready for their return trip, Joseph had more surprises for them. This time not only was the money for the grain returned, but Joseph's personal silver goblet was hidden in Benjamin's sack. Giving the brothers an opportunity to leave, Joseph then sent an Egyptian security unit after them. It soon overtook them and accused them of taking the goblet. Thinking that none of them had stolen it, the brothers agreed that should it be found among the possessions of any of them, that one would become Joseph's slave.

In the confrontation that followed the goblet's discovery, Judah showed himself to be of heroic stature. Requesting the privilege of addressing Joseph, he spoke eloquently of the brothers' problem (44:18-34): to leave Benjamin behind would be to insure their father's death. Instead of Benjamin, he offered himself as Joseph's slave. Unable to control his feelings any longer, Joseph ordered the room cleared of all except his brothers. Then, bursting into tears, he revealed himself to them.

The story of Joseph and his brothers is highly complex. Filled with negative elements of greed, suspicion, and hatred, it ends in an emotion-packed scene of reconciliation. Obviously this story contains important clues to understanding the process of forgiveness, if only we can identify them.

Joseph's behavior is at once a source of confusion and a clue to understanding. At first glance Joseph's choices of action seem to indicate a mean and vicious spirit. He had his brothers where he wanted them. By holding Simeon hostage and demanding that Benjamin accompany them, he raised their anxiety level close to the point of overflow. He does not appear to have been bent on forgiveness so much as on repayment for the evil done to him in the past.

Certain clues take us beyond such an interpretation, however. One is that we know that Joseph had been separated from his brothers for a long time. He no doubt had very painful memories of having been rejected by them. Yet his early questioning of them gave evidence of a genuinely deep concern for his entire family. They may have rejected him, but he had not rejected them. They were a part of his family, and he demonstrated his loyalty to that family.

Further, Joseph's evident toughness toward his brothers may very well have been necessary to the healing process.

For two parties to be reconciled they need to meet at the point of the pain. Occasionally someone will ask for forgiveness and be answered, "Sure. It's OK. It wasn't really important." That is to deny the pain and to reject the feelings of the one seeking forgiveness. The breach in the relationship is only scabbed over, and no real healing can occur. By handling it the way he did, Joseph could demonstrate the depth of pain he had experienced and also determine the capacity of the brothers to be in touch with their father's pain.

Throughout human history individuals have never found it difficult to learn behavior and acquire attitudes that destroy family unity. As each family member struggles to achieve and maintain a personal identity, the corporate nature of the family is placed under enormous stress. As persons are forced to live together in close proximity, and as they are asked to share an intimate existence, painful and disruptive encounters are nearly inevitable. Individual differences looking for an opportunity for expression offer a tremendous challenge.

That hurt should happen and family unity become splintered is not surprising. The main lesson we can learn from Jacob's family is that assessing blame and pinpointing the reason for breakup is not as important as a willingness to enter into the forgiveness process.

A confrontation of persons involved is a necessity if they are to experience the full measure of forgiveness. In that confrontation the parties involved must become aware of each other—truly aware of pain caused and experienced. Then they must share the pain to the fullest dimension. To say "I'm sorry" without genuinely entering into the pain of the other person involved is empty and does nothing to restore unity and oneness. There is no cheap grace; there is no painless forgiveness. Broken relationships are painful and are only restored through the experience of suffering.

One brother, other than Joseph, becomes especially memorable. We can watch him grow through his lifetime into a mature and caring family member. That brother is

Judah, and his speech, recorded in chapter 44, is a truly beautiful expression. His offering to become a slave in place of Benjamin in order to protect his father from more pain demonstrates Judah's awareness of the meaning of love and his willingness to enter into an experience of sacrificial love. We see something of the character that became evident in the one chosen to continue the line of God's people.

Questions for Reflection

1. Consider the elements in the final reconciliation of Joseph and his brothers. Was it important to decide who was at fault? Why?

2. In your own experience or that of your family, what role has crisis played in the effecting of a reconciliation?

3. What about the choice to live by principle? Where does the principle of "an eye for an eye and a tooth for a tooth" fit with the element of reconciliation? If you choose to live by principles, how do you select the principles?

4. How would you find out whether you could now trust someone who had caused you suffering in the past? How important is it to make that assessment?

5. Think about the following sentence in relation to the crucifixion of Christ: "Broken relationships are painful and are only restored through the experience of suffering." In what way is Judah's willingness to take the place of Benjamin similar to Jesus' willingness to die in our place?

12

Jacob's Farewell

Genesis 46–49

Chapter 46 through the end of the book contains the record of the final days of Jacob and Joseph. With God's permission they resided in Egypt as a family. Joseph was there as a result of the hatred of his brothers. Jacob chose to go there to be reunited with Joseph and to escape the ravages of a severe famine.

Chapter 46 begins with a reiteration of the major theme of Genesis. Before Jacob entered Egypt, he chose to stop off to worship at Beersheba. The implication is that he needed reassurance of God's continued protection. Not only did God give that reassurance, but once more God stated the promise that had been given earlier to Jacob's father and grandfather. The message was this:

'I am God, the God of your father. Do not be afraid to go down to Egypt, for there I will make you a great nation. I will go down with you to Egypt, and I myself will bring you back again without fail; and Joseph shall close your eyes' (vv. 3-4).

God was calling a people into being. Jacob was an instrument for fulfilling that purpose. A temporary sojourn in Egypt

79

did not invalidate Jacob's role in that plan. Jacob could go to Egypt knowing that he would not leave God behind.

Our understanding of Jacob's need and God's response to that need is particularly important for our age. In our society we are transient people who have often lost touch with our extended families. To move from place to place is to lose our sense of rootedness. We need a reminder that God is not tied to a particular locality or to some specific ritual. We need to be reminded that we belong to the people of God, that we are part of God's continuing creative work in the world. If we listen to this reiteration of God's promise and hear it directed to us personally, we can have some deep needs met.

Following this experience of reassurance for Jacob, the Bible lists the names of his sons. That list reminds us that God was fulfilling the promise to multiply this family and make of it a great people. In God's continued relationship with his Chosen People there was to be a significant change. A patriarch of the people of God was entering Egypt with several of his sons. God would be going with them into the land. Later, after they had multiplied many times over, God would lead them from Egypt to a land of their own.

When the sons of Jacob settled in Egypt, they found an immediate vocational opening. Being a shepherd was not a high-status profession for Egyptians, and so the Israelites became shepherds. Joseph not only continued in a role of power but shrewdly increased that power, becoming even more influential with the pharaoh. Jacob grew old knowing that his children were well cared for in every way.

As Jacob grew old, he prepared for his death. In that preparation a rather curious event occurred between him and Joseph. First, the two sons of Joseph were given full standing with their uncles. Then, appearing before Jacob, now nearly blind, they were carefully arranged by Joseph so that the elder would be given a special blessing. Just as carefully, Jacob refused to be controlled, and he reversed the blessing process. That this has some special significance to the Israelites in their historical perspective seems to be a logical interpretation. What it teaches us today is not so clear.

When Jacob summoned all of his sons for the final blessing, one of the characteristics of the people of God was stated once more and emphasized. Chapter 49 is a song of farewell, the theme of which is a celebration of the individual differences brought together in one family. The brothers were different in ways that did not encourage family unity. The song reminded them that their expressions of individuality had not always been appropriate or proper. Still they were one family called of God to become the people through whom God would reveal himself to all of humanity. As we listen to this farewell song of Jacob, we once again hear the message of the grace of God. How else can we explain that this motley assortment of lustful, violent, phlegmatic, yet often beautiful people can be brought together for such a noble purpose?

It probably will help our understanding to look briefly at the sons of Jacob through their father's eyes. Reuben is seen as so lustful that he does not always honor his father's bed. Simeon and Levi are violent men given to impulsive and murderous actions. More attention is paid to Judah, who is courageous and will be the one carrying the royal line. Zebulun will dwell by the seashore welcoming ships that sail the seas. Issachar is a phlegmatic beast of burden. Dan and Gad will live in constant conflict with neighboring peoples. Asher will be known as a creative chef. Naphtali is simply described as a beautiful tree. Joseph is described in lyrical terms that tell of his persistence and strength, and much blessing is called down for him from God. Very briefly, Benjamin is called, "a ravening wolf."

The sons of Jacob represent a wide variety of humanity. They are remarkably human in their strengths and weakness. Together they form the family chosen as the people of God. By the grace of God they corporately represent God and keep God's name before the world.

Jacob's farewell blessing is poignant, lyrical, and challenging to us. Who are those who are members of the people of God today? They are very human people like you and me with an assortment of weaknesses and strengths. One thing we share in common: the grace of God. As recipients of grace we share our individual humanity so that corporately we may bear witness to the presence of God in the world.

Questions for Reflection

1. If economic conditions should force you to move from your home church, how would your faith enter into the experience?

2. Review the account of Jacob and of Joseph and his brothers, noting the occasions in which the grace of God is especially evident. How could you define the grace of God?

3. What diversity is present among the members of your church congregation? How is such diversity in your church brought together to be a corporate expression of the grace of God?

4. In what ways does your church congregation encourage diversity of thinking and responding?

13

Burial in Egypt

Genesis 50

The last days of Joseph are recorded in chapter 50. Of first concern in the record is the proper burial of Jacob. Considerable attention is given to the account. Details are included that demonstrate Joseph's importance among the Egyptians and, along with that importance, his complete devotion to his racial and religious heritage.

Jacob's embalming utilized the full knowledge and ceremonial emphasis of the Egyptians. We are told the process took forty days, "the usual time for embalming" (v. 2). There was a period of national mourning for seventy days, and then the body was transported back to the Israelite country. The trip back to Canaan was impressive, involving "all Pharaoh's courtiers, the elders of his household, and all the elders of Egypt, together with all Joseph's own household . . ." (v. 7). Not surprisingly, such an entourage created some considerable stir among the Canaanites.

With this remarkable event we can see an important period in the experience of the people of God coming to an end. The emphasis has been upon the patriarchs. Abraham, Isaac, Jacob, and Joseph were men with very human characteristics, through whom the people of God were called into being. As the last of the patriarchs, Joseph reflected something of a transition. After Joseph died, the way was cleared for a new emphasis. We are now ready to witness an emerging corporateness. Great leaders like Moses, Joshua, and David will appear on the scene, but the focus will be basically on the people in their corporate experience before God.

In this last chapter of the book, Joseph's character is clearly on display. Not only did he show respect for his father's wishes, but he also showed his desire to maintain continuity with the family's heritage. Jacob's body was taken to the "cave on the plot of land at Machpelah, the land which Abraham had bought as a burial place . . . " (v. 13), which was in the land of the family's origin. Though the family's fortunes were now combined with those of Egypt, there was in Jacob's command to be buried in Canaan a recognition that the relationship with Egypt was temporary. The destiny of this family and this emerging people would be as a separate people who owed nothing to other nations. The only dependency they would acknowledge for any period of time would be upon God. The mark of this people was its unique relationship to God.

The temporary nature of the family sojourn found emphatic statement in Joseph's final orders before his death. Recorded in verses 24 and 25, his words reflect the importance of God's call to the people and of God's promise to them. Even his burying place was temporary. His embalmed body was placed in a coffin ready to be transported back to the homeland when the time came for departure from Egypt.

Along with the death and burial of Jacob and Joseph, chapter 50 contains one other family vignette. Recorded in verses 15 through 21 is the account of the brothers' fear of Joseph after Jacob died. Though Joseph had previously expressed his forgiveness to them, the brothers were not certain that he would not turn on them and destroy them. Once more, a word from Joseph was required to alleviate their still unresolved guilt and assure them of his continuing concern.

This incident reminds us of the tremendous significance of forgiveness in maintaining family harmony. It further testifies to the great difficulty in understanding the nature and meaning of forgiveness. Forgiveness is that experience meant to restore a broken relationship. Forgiveness is not some sort of trade-off by which an evil deed is matched with a good deed. Forgiveness becomes fully complete when both parties in the experience accept that past events no longer control them and that the relationship has begun again with a fresh new start. This was no problem for Joseph; it was more difficult for his brothers. We can understand their problem. To receive forgiveness from one whom we have wronged is still a nearly overwhelming experience.

Questions for Reflection

1. In chapter 50, verses 15-21, an interesting regression among Joseph's brothers is described. What does this tell you about the difficulty of accepting forgiveness? When is the forgiveness experience completed?

2. Though we might protest that our dependency is only on God, we may find we are relying upon some others too heavily. Identify these persons.

3. What do you think of a parent ordering a child to tell someone that he or she is sorry? In what way does this prepare children to learn the process of forgiveness?

4. What should a person do if another attempts to reconcile a fractured relationship too quickly or too cheaply?

5. Can you think of a brother or sister or friend from whom you have become estranged? What steps can you take toward reconciliation? What might be a source of pain if those steps were taken?

14

An Emerging People Who Live by Faith

W e have worked our way through the book of Genesis. We began our journey with an understanding that this was the Word of God. We have tried to demonstrate that in this book we can hear God speaking to us with a message that will be meaningful to us in our current life situations. What has been said here by way of interpretation is clearly only a beginning. We hope that those who have come this far have learned a process for listening and will be able to find further messages from rereading the book of Genesis.

What is in order now is to identify a bit more clearly one or two of the major themes appearing in the book. By seeing them more clearly as they appear here, we can find them more easily in the remainder of the Bible. Further, we will be able to grasp their meaning for us in our response to a personal God.

The theme that, for this writer at least, has the greatest significance in the total biblical context is that of the emerging people of God. Here is the beginning of the delineation of this theme. Here we find some of the theme's most important elements. Here we can see these elements in a simple form that will be an introduction to a more complex development occurring later in the Bible.

The foundation for this theme is God's act of creation. By God's word the world came into being. Out of chaos and nothingness came order and substance. The crown of that creation was humanity. To be a human being is to possess special privileges and to bear great responsibility. Humanity carries the image of God ("Let us make man in our image and likeness . . . ") and is responsible for maintaining order (" . . . to rule the fish in the sea, the birds of the heaven, the cattle, all wild animals on earth, and all the reptiles that crawl upon the earth"). How humanity responds to the privileges and carries the responsibilities becomes a basic biblical issue and something of profound importance for our life today.

An implication in this description of creation is that humanity is to occupy a special place in relationship to the Creator. Freedom of choice in the relationship is a basic element. This demands intentionality on the part of members of humanity. A member of the human race is free to choose to accept God's sovereignty and live according to God's will, or he or she can choose to resist that will. In this setting making no choice is choosing resistance and rebellion.

Choosing to live according to the will of God is choosing to live in community. That part of God's will is revealed in the nature of creation. Humanity comes in two forms—male and female. Both need the other to be complete. The choice to live in community begets further choices concerned with how one incomplete individual shares that incompleteness in a way that results in the wholeness of community.

No larger challenge exists for us than creating community. Individualistic existence may have looked like a viable option some time back in history. It certainly is not attractive today. As a result of the population explosion and modern technology we live in closer proximity to our neighbors than ever before. If we must live closely *alongside* of these other representatives of humanity, common sense would indicate that we look for ways to live *with* them. If there is some

solution for living together and thus experiencing wholeness, we need to bend every effort to find it.

The beginning experiences of community as recorded in
Genesis bring encouragement to us. Community does not,
in the final analysis, exist because we make it happen. Community comes into being because God wills it to be so. God
works in the face of human resistance. God succeeds in
spite of human stubbornness, human rebellion, human ignorance, or human failure.

That community does not depend on conformity among
its members. Unity is not the result of every member looking like every other member. Differences among the members are welcomed and celebrated. Both male and female
are needed; cowboys and farmers are to live side by side.
An individual member is not swallowed up by the community but finds purpose and fulfillment within community.
Wholeness for humanity is the result. Humanity is meant
to be more than the sum of its individual parts.

What we see unfolding in the Genesis account is a mode
of operation. God is at work, and God works in a particular
way, using consistent methods and a clearly definable spirit.
What will become incarnate in Jesus of Nazareth is already
at work in this beginning era. Here is revealed a God of
great compassion. Here can be seen the grace of God at
work. Grace identified as compassion calls a people into
being; grace identified as forgiveness maintains and perpetuates the existence of that people. The theological con-
cept of grace can be discussed and even eulogized. As we
see it described in the lives and experiences of humans—
even those who lived many hundreds of years before us—
we can grasp the meaning of grace and appropriate it for
our own lives.

In the beginning God was at work creating a world and
creating humans to live in that world. This creator God is
described as a personal God desiring relationships with personal beings whom he has created. For that desire to be
fulfilled, human creation must choose to live according to

God's will, which means to choose to live in community. When that choice is made, humans become personal and are prepared to enter into relationship with a personal God.

That part has been discussed previously in this book. Moving on from this point, let us look at another important theme that is introduced in the book of Genesis. God is at work in the world, but he remains outside the limits of this world. He is not limited to his world, and he is no way subject to demands from within that world. Though God has chosen to give dominion over the rest of creation to human beings, he does not abdicate his sovereignty. He desires humans to relate to him personally, but that relationship will be on his terms.

All of this is a prelude to the introduction of the new biblical theme: humans relate to God through faith. God cannot be fully defined nor sensorially confined. The five senses are important for humans in relating to one another. They are of secondary importance in relating to God. God is beyond our sensory limitations and must be known only in an attitude of trust that takes us beyond those limitations.

Faith does not, as the little boy in Sunday church school described it, have us believe something even when we know it isn't true. Faith challenges us to live today knowing that tomorrow is in the hands of the unseen God. Faith gives us the resources to act in the right way even though that action carries an apparent threat to our existence. Faith opens the door for God's intervention in human affairs.

How does Genesis teach about faith? Faith finds expression in the lives of the major characters in the Genesis narrative, from Abraham and Sarah on through Joseph. When Abraham acted in obedience to the call of God by going to a new and unfamiliar land, faith became a primary and much desired human characteristic. Abraham became a hero of faith because he *acted* on the best revelation of the will of God that he possessed. Without a money-back guarantee he chose the path of obedience.

As we watch faith as a life force unfolding in the lives of

Abraham, Sarah, Isaac, Jacob, and Joseph, we learn some extremely important lessons for our own lives. Faith is not a magic charm to ward off evil. It is not something that enters a human life and immediately permeates all that a person does. Faith is a mind-set that begins to take one deeper and deeper into a relationship with the personal God. Faith begins in obedient action and leads to a serenity of spirit.

What is it to live by faith? Learning from the book of Genesis, we discover that living by faith is choosing to live without standard human security symbols ("Leave your own country, your kinsmen, and your father's house, and go to a country that I will show you"). Faith hears God getting the last laugh over doubt. Living by faith means constantly reassessing one's values and priorities. Always, living by faith is acting on one's best understanding of right and wrong even when one is a stranger and captive in a foreign land.

Beyond what has been stated, faith opens one to a deepening understanding of life's meaning. Growth is depicted as coming through experiences when mistakes are made, but new understanding results from facing up to and owning these mistakes. Thus Abraham can palm off Sarah as his sister, Sarah can laugh at God, and Jacob can wrong his brother. Perhaps the most important aspect for our time is that living in faith can lead to reconciliation between brothers and sisters.

Faith won't bring God into our personal life arena. It will not allow us to insure getting what we want from God. What faith does is to take us up into the will and purposes of God. As we grow in faith, we are taken beyond a life confined and limited to the five senses. Faith is our entrance into eternity.

The people of God are those called by God to trust him and to express that trust in obedience. The people of God are those who live by faith. In that trusting commitment to the will of God, each individual member can become open to the other. Entrance into the wholeness of community is the result.

Questions for Reflection

1. In what ways do you experience membership in the emerging people of God?

2. What does it mean to you that you are in the image of God?

3. To what extent have you chosen to live "in community"?

4. Review your own pilgrimage of faith. At what times have you given up some form of security to step out in faith? What mistakes have you made that led to growth? What values and priorities have you changed in light of deepening understanding of God's will, purpose, and grace?

5. How deep is your trust in God? How deeply do you trust the community of faith? How does trust in God and community of faith find expression in your life?

15

New Beginnings

The book of Genesis is the book of beginnings. In poetic and profound fashion these fifty chapters describe God's creation of our world and the calling into being of a people. Fifty chapters are hardly sufficient for the task. They are not meant to be a definitive statement or a complete account. The book is intended to be a point of beginning in understanding the nature of our humanity. As such, this book can be of tremendous value in finding our individual places on the human scene.

As I wrote, I deliberately avoided footnotes and references to commentaries. I value good commentaries and use them regularly. They can, however, take us from a direct encounter with the Bible. I want persons to be introduced to the Bible, and I want them to be encouraged to listen to the living God speak through the Bible. What has been written here was intended to be a model for those willing to struggle with this immensely important communication process.

So look again at how these words can speak to you. Turn to this book with an open mind. Don't allow yourself to become entangled with old debates that say little about your practical needs right now. A new beginning for you might be to think through what the experience of Adam and Eve can tell you about your sin. What is it for you to be "like God"? Where do you find yourself resisting being simply what God created you to be? Do you ever catch yourself attempting to be something other than human and thus putting yourself in danger of being less than human?

Move on from Adam and Eve to Cain and Abel. Quite likely you haven't been guilty of murdering your sibling. Does that take Cain and Abel out of the realm of your personal experience? Not necessarily. How do you approach those who are different from you? Are you inclined to fear them and thus build barriers between them and you?

As a pastor I am often asked, "How can I know the will of God for my life?" There are, of course, no simple answers to this complex question. I can, however, help the individual questioner sort out items of personal data, like age, educational preparation, and personal gifts. I can ask them to reflect on how they see the world's needs. Then I can direct them to some basic biblical principles, many of which are present in the book of Genesis.

The book of Genesis clearly teaches that the will of God concerns human wholeness expressed through living in community. Any personal function or role will be in the direction of harmonious living. Any private call that works toward disharmony within the created order is suspect. Any message that advocates or perpetuates a social order consisting of superior and inferior beings should be questioned. The will of God for one's life is in the direction of healing, reconciliation, and an ultimate unity.

I invite you to begin again with your own Bible reading. Begin again with the book of beginnings. Find a contemporary translation that will read smoothly. If you start to bog down in the genealogy lists, skip them. Stay with the narrative. Use your imagination to put yourself close to the action. Stay in touch with your feelings as you read. Rejoice with Sarah when Isaac is born. Wrestle with the matter of ultimate loyalty along with Abraham. Hurt with the family members of Jacob as the family is divided and threatened by famine. Be willing to let your own tears flow in the awesomeness of family reconciliation as Joseph forgives his brothers.

I am extending this invitation to read the Bible especially to those of you who haven't read it for some time or perhaps have never read it consistently. Take your Bible off the shelf and dust it off. Then look to see what version it is. If it is the King James Version, put it back on the shelf temporarily. That translation was done in 1611, and unless you have had some good training in reading the English of Shakespeare's time, you won't find it very easy going. If the King James Version is the only translation you have, invest in any of the newer translations. Don't read verse by verse or even chapter by chapter. Read each event completely through.

What can you expect to learn from reading the book of Genesis? Without much effort you can discover that the ways in which humans have attempted to live together haven't changed very much through the centuries. Some persons still think that the way to cope with human difference is to destroy those who are different. Even today there are those who, like Abraham and Lot, are content to maintain a peaceful coexistence. A marked improvement over the Cain approach, it is still far short of the Joseph approach. There are some who, like Joseph, see the importance of maintaining the ties of the human family and will risk rejection and painful separation to do so. These are the people who have struggled deeply with the meaning of forgiveness.

I invite you to begin again to listen for the living God to speak to you through the Bible. Listening to God, you can be directed in a path that can lead you to being fully human. To be all one can be is hardly a dull exercise. This is what God wants for you: to be all you can be in relation to your Creator. That possibility is well worth working toward.

Questions for Reflection

1. Having listened for God to speak to you through the book of Genesis, where will you turn now for further guidance? What other book of the Bible seems particularly appealing?

2. If the Bible does have significance for our present-day living, sharing the reading of it makes good sense. What Bible-study groups are there in your congregation? What will you look for in a Bible-study group?